ANSWERS
from a
GRANDER SELF

Edited by TAM MOSSMAN

TIGER
MAPLE
PRESS

CAVE CREEK, ARIZONA

**For Susan
who's always there,
even when I'm not**

. . .

CONTENTS

The bridge between worlds is built eternally and, even as a spider's web, derives its strength and efficiency from being constantly restructured.

— *James*

ANSWERS

FROM

A

GRANDER

SELF

A NOTE TO THE READER

Today, you can find channeled materials (or "spirit writings," as the Library of Congress calls them) in almost any bookstore. There are serious surveys of the phenomenon (notably Arthur Hastings's *With the Tongues of Men and Angels*). Magazines such as *Connecting Link* and *Spirit Speaks* print channeled articles. Still not satisfied? There are even do-it-yourself "guide" books on contacting a entity of your very own.

It wasn't always so. Back in 1984, a computer-graphics artist named Mark Zweigler visited me in Philadelphia to show me *The Jacob Sessions*, a series of essays dictated to him in trance. They were first-rate, I assured him—but warned that he'd have trouble finding a publisher: Edgar Cayce and Jane Roberts had virtually divided the "Occult" bookshelf between them. Editors weren't at all receptive to Johnny (and Joanie)-come-latelies.

Besides Mark, I knew of several other people who were receiving fascinating material and getting nothing but rejection slips for their pains. True, some of their trance personalities spouted near-drivel from time to time—but so did living authors! Why discriminate against the disembodied?

It was Mark's *Jacob Sessions* that pushed me over the edge. Convinced that top-quality writing—of whatever origin—deserved a hearing, I founded *Metapsychology* (dauntingly subtitled *The Journal of Discarnate Intelligence*) and mailed out 200 copies of the first issue in May, 1985.

From the outset, I invited subscribers to submit questions for "our" discarnates to answer. No topic was taboo, as long as long as the question was of general interest. All incoming queries were collated and mailed out to channels across the United States and Canada—whose trance personalities decided which questions, if any, *they* wanted to answer. The most insightful of their replies were printed in the Questions & Answers section of each issue.

Within a year, *Meta*'s circulation had climbed to 1,800. I kept trying to showcase as many talented "voices" as possible —yet some of the most thought-provoking material came from an entity I channeled myself, while sitting at an electric typewriter in a fourth-floor office overlooking the Schuylkill River.

❖

My involvement with this whole phenomenon began in 1968: Less than a year after Prentice-Hall hired me as an Assistant Editor, I was handed a slush-pile manuscript to read and evaluate. In it, a writer named Jane Roberts—published author of *How to Develop Your ESP Power*—made frustratingly brief references to a personality named Seth whom she'd contacted through the Ouija board.

I wrote Ms. Roberts. Would she be interested in writing a book that focused on Seth and what he had to say? Ms. Roberts was! That September, I drove up to meet her in Elmira, NY.

You'll find me disguised me as "Matt, the editor from New York" in Chapter 11 of *The Seth Material*. Our first visit convinced me that Seth was a separate entity in his own right—especially since I seemed to sense him as an independent presence. I could feel his energy gathering in the room, like the restless tension in the air before a thunderstorm breaks.

Seth Material sold only modestly, but *Seth Speaks*, published two years later, really took off. During subsequent visits, as Jane's shelf of published books grew wider and wider, I had many opportunities to watch Jane glide in and out of trance. To me, her mediumship seemed a breathtaking gift that—like composing music or calculating square roots in one's head—lay far beyond my reach.

Then one muggy night in 1975, I drove to Brooklyn to visit a friend I'll call Greg, who'd been honing his psychic abilities since he was a teenager. Now, after dinner, we lingered at the table, sipping wine and swapping personal experiences, theories, and frustrations. All at once, I felt my consciousness being "dimmed," as if my brain was hooked up to a rheostat that someone was slowly, gently twisting toward OFF. The experience should have been alarming, but I felt comfortable—almost snug! I told Greg that I wanted to see where this sensation would lead me . . . but if I drifted down into insensibility, would he please reel me back?

My awareness continued to narrow. Somehow, physical space seemed to flatten in on itself, as if miles of distance had folded themselves up and were stacked directly in front of my closed eyes. Idly, I remembered having felt something like this when I was very young, just before falling asleep.

Words began to "arrive," one by one. I repeated them out loud, in sequence. It was like watching a flashlight beam crawl across a large-print billboard: I was aware of each phrase as I voiced it, but had no idea what words were coming next.

My voice took on a new, distinctive accent, and Greg realized he was listening to a trance personality. "Can I ask who you are?"

Our surprise visitor claimed to be "Tam's higher self," but said that he didn't define himself with a name. "Well," sighed Greg, "We have to call you something. How about James?"

The entity nodded—and so, he's been James ever since.

His first appearance was relatively brief—no more than ten or fifteen minutes. James used the time to analyze Greg's relationship with his girlfriend, Linda. By allowing themselves too many possible outs, James warned, they were eroding the strength of their commitment, just as—in his analogy—too many escape hatches would weaken the hull of a submarine.

About a year later, Greg and Linda did indeed break up. And by then, I'd learned that my experiences with James were by no means unique. The entity's reluctance to confine himself with a name; his eerie ability to answer unspoken questions; my ensuing amnesia of what he said—in the accounts of other trance mediums, such details cropped up again and again.

For the next nine years—partly because I didn't want to be accused of imitating Jane Roberts, whose trances were obviously much deeper than mine—I did little to explore my contact with James, aside from letting him through to speak one-on-one with people who wanted his advice. Even then, I never bothered to record what he said.

Finally, in 1984, a friend in Alexandria, VA asked if I would Amtrak down and let James take questions from a live audience. I said I'd give it a try, even if I couldn't promise that James would show up. But I needn't have worried. That evening, in a light but firm trance, I enjoyed the satisfaction of feeling James's words click together to form sentences. Now and again, I'd be startled by audience laughter and dimly realize that James had cracked a joke.

Leafing through transcripts of this session gave me a better sense of James's conversational strategies. When I feared that he was digressing, actually James had been dollying back to frame his topic in a wider context. Also, he took obvious

pleasure in piquing curiosity and clearing away misunderstand-
ings. Typically, he'd take a question apart before answering it,
gently showing where its hidden assumptions were too
narrow for the answer he wanted to give.

Later, to publicize *Metapsychology*, I made James available
to audiences in Philadelphia, Honolulu, Ottawa, Denver, Chicago,
and other cities. Many of his answers, I realized, would
make great fodder for the magazine, but transcribing the
cassette tapes was a slow and painstaking chore.

Happily, while preparing the first issue of the Journal
for the typesetter, I found a much simpler way of getting
James's replies on paper. Feeling the inner pressure that meant
he wanted to communicate, I'd prime myself with a deep cup
of strong black coffee and sit down at that electric typewriter.
Almost immediately his words would start flowing in my
mind's ear, and I would type them down as fast as I could.

For example, when I began taking down his explanation
of the mechanics of channeling (here reprinted in Chapter 1),
I had no idea how long it would be. I filled five double-spaced
pages, then felt James pause—and naturally assumed he was
finished. But no: He went on to dictate a long block of text,
then asked that it be inserted on page 5—where, to my astonish-
ment, it fit perfectly!

All of James's longer essays "arrived" this way, at a single
sitting—and were perfectly polished and organized. Only my
errors of transcription need fixing before such "typewriter
trance" material went to the printer.

I didn't want to spotlight James at the expense of other
entities, so getting enough representative material for each issue
of *Meta* meant wading through hundreds of pages of yet-unpub-
lished trance sessions from across the U.S. and Canada. I couldn't
help noticing that some "name-brand" entities (whose weekend
seminars cost hundreds of dollars to attend) seemed repetitious
and needlessly wordy. Others sounded trite and unoriginal, as if
they'd cribbed from Wayne Dyer or Norman Vincent Peale. Still
others held forth on arcane topics of apparent interest to *them*,
but not terribly useful for those trying to live in the material
world. Reading their uneven output only increased my good
opinion of James.

Can I really be objective about his material? Yes, because while delivering it, I'm only marginally aware of it—and usually forget it a few minutes afterwards. When I finally get to read it or hear it on tape, weeks—sometimes even months —have elapsed. James's rolling, elegant, old-fashioned style is so different from mine that I react to it as someone else's work.

Re-reading my own prose, I'm always finding lost opportunities where I could have improved it. With James, that's not so— I can read his essays over and over with undiminished pleasure.

Like most fledgling magazines, *Metapsychology* lost money, and after twelve issues, I had to close it down. Not long after, a Kansas City publisher asked me to assemble James's material into book form. James dictated nine chapter titles (in no particular order), and I started leafing through old transcripts and back issues of *Metapsychology* for answers to fit under each heading. His answers—which had seemed random and disjointed, a metaphysical grab-bag—quickly gathered into rich clusters, their insights augmenting and clarifying one another. I could see an actual book taking shape! As soon as I realized that James's discussion of evil could stand on its own, as a separate chapter, the rest of his answers and essays neatly arranged themselves under the headings he'd already provided.

The publisher was delighted with the manuscript of *Answers from a Grander Self*—but went bankrupt before he could set it into type. Kindly, he released me from my contract. I promptly signed with a Indianapolis firm who planned to feature *Answers* as their lead title. This time, the book made it as far as camera-ready page proofs (the last stage before printing and binding) before the publisher ran out of money!

Still optimistic, I mailed off photocopies of those page proofs to various New-Age editors who asked to see them— and who, I expected, would welcome a twice-contracted book that was already copyedited, typeset and ready to go.

All of them turned it down.

The last straw was a letter from a Manhattan publishing house that had been sitting on *Answers* for many months. "I loved it," their Associate Editor admitted, "but as often happens with controversial topics, I couldn't rally enough support for it. In other words, since my colleagues don't buy the premise, they couldn't get behind the book."

Based on my other rejection letters, I suspect the real problem wasn't James's "controversial" premise, but the poor sales history of other, similar books.

In economics, Gresham's Law states that bad money (paper greenbacks, base-metal coinage with no intrinsic worth) drives good money (gold and silver) out of circulation. So too, in publishing: When a book fails to sell, editors take a dim view of any roughly similar project—even a good one. Throughout the '80s, too many mediocre channeled works were published, with too few readers willing to sort wheat from chaff. Prentice-Hall, Jane Roberts's long-term publisher, had kept her books in print for nearly 20 years. But in 1991, faced with declining sales, they put most of her work out of print.

Why, then, am I self-publishing *Answers*? Didn't I learn my lesson with *Meta*? With more than enough glop and treacle out there, why underwrite yet another dose of *samizdat* from the beyond? Quite simply, that editor's "I loved it" convinces me there's something here after all. If *Answers* succeeds, it won't be the first time I've had to sneak a worthy manuscript past the unresponsive and the unimaginative: At Prentice-Hall, I contracted my first best selling book, *W. C. Fields & Me*, after 22 other publishers (including my immediate superior!) had rejected it.

Okay, but why is *this* book worth reading? Because I think James has important things to say—and says them in a language that even non-mystics can understand.

Given free rein and a book to fill, trance personalities can become abstract and theoretical. So can James, in his still unfinished *Private Allegories and the Nature of Personal Symbolism*. Here, what keeps him lively and relevant is the down-to-earth quality of the questions he chose to tackle.

A quick skim of the following pages will show you just what I mean. Very few questioners try to flaunt their knowledge or sound superior (and when they do, James lets them off easy). Most ask wistful, modest, Why-can't-I-astral-project? type questions . . . theoretical When-does-reincarnation-end? questions . . . blunt, angry, Why-is-there-AIDS? questions . . . hushed, fearful, Are-Satanists-taking-over-the-world? questions . . . in short, the kind of untrimmed, honest, meat-and-potatoes queries that people *really* want answered—and have been asking, stubbornly, for hundreds and hundreds of years.

And James responds in kind. His answers are compassionate, clear, and above all *practical*, telling you step-by-step how to lose excess weight, earn more money, replace bad habits, make your home safe from disaster, recall your dreams, and achieve your creative top potential (in any field!)—while handling your doubts and objections along the way. On the rare occasions where James accepts a strictly personal, Should-I-dump-my-spouse-for-my-old-boyfriend? type question, it's fascinating to eavesdrop while he plays Ann Landers, dispensing sane, common-sense advice.

Even if you don't buy the premise, you can *still* get behind the book.

❖

Readers of Jane Roberts will notice that James uses a number of terms and concepts originally coined by Seth. But that only makes sense: Jane Roberts's work largely molded my own metaphysical thinking; and after her death in 1984, many who had whetted their curiosity on those same books came to James with their follow-up questions.

Nevertheless, James goes on to break important new ground. As far as I can determine, his explanation of how we gather "extra–sensory" knowledge—through resonance, assumption, and the intermediary mode—is wholly original. His concept of adjacent lives makes better sense of reincarnation by giving our so-called "past" selves a dynamic and far more fluid role in our present existence.

What becomes of us after death? According to James, our earthly personalities are propelled along several different (but simultaneous) avenues of personal evolution. Each of us is both the offshoot *and* the seed of an enormous, self-aware aggregate of consciousness—what Jane Roberts termed the Source Self or Oversoul, and which James calls a Grander Self. Fortunately, I don't have to paraphrase his banyan-tree analogy; it's all there in Chapter 9.

Seth tirelessly repeated that "You create your own reality," but James begins to explain exactly how we accomplish that nifty feat! My wife, Susan, and I routinely turn back to answers that James delivered years ago to make sense of our day-to-day experience. For us, at least, his theories fit the "facts" of life more accurately than any other explanations we've read.

❖

Back when I was publishing *Meta*, I endured letters from a rabid skeptic who accused me of putting on an act, of creating an imaginary persona named James for fun and profit. If James was really a separate entity, why didn't people perceive him independently?

Well, they do! At 1988 Psi-Day in Lynchburg, VA, I asked the audience to tell me if they saw anything unusual during James's presentation. Afterwards, a woman reported seeing a yellow light bobbing above my head before I went into trance. From time to time, others have perceived James as a triangular shape or as a tall human-shaped silhouette—but invariably, yellow in color.

And while I can't prove that James is what he claims to be, I can offer pretty solid evidence for what he is *not*.

Back in 1985, psychologist Michael Sussman, then based in Philadelphia, set out to analyze James's personality and compare it with mine. Over two days, he subjected each of us to the same battery of tests—Rorschach, Thematic Apperception, and Sentence Completion, among others. After the results came in, Michael wrote to assure me that my "test results and clinical interview did *not* indicate Multiple Personality Disorder or any psychotic process." (Whew!)

"I.Q. testing revealed no significant differences quantitatively between you and James. However, both sets of scores were in the upper range (Very Superior), and the Wechsler Test does not discriminate well between scores at either extreme.

"Qualitatively, there were indications of different styles of thinking and speech. Projective tests strongly indicated two separate personalities. The most striking difference was that you showed tendencies toward depression, while James showed strong tendencies toward manic behavior and thought."

I can see why: On a multiple-choice test, he indicated his sex as *both* M and F, and ignored mundane questions like "I read the newspaper every morning—true or false?" When Michael asked him the population of the U.S., he said (I *think* jokingly) "Let me do my own count." Asked to draw a tree, he sketched a stylized sapling bearing flowers on the left and fruit on the right, then signed the page with a glyph that resembled Babylonian cuneiform.

❖

Whatever James's origin or essence, he constantly churns out insights and explanations I could never arrive at on my own. Often he'll refer to specific events in his listeners' private pasts—of which I know absolutely ziltch. And even some of his outlandish claims eventually pan out. In 1981, for example, he told a New Jersey woman that she was "two people in one," the product of two fertilized eggs that had combined into a single fetus.

To me, the idea sounded medically impossible—until I read the Spring 1988 issue of *Rotunda*, a Canadian magazine. It reported an identical case that had been confirmed by doctors in Austria: "Although [the woman's] blood was type AB, one of her children had type O. That's not possible in the straight-forward inheritance of blood groups . . . It was also shown that the woman's parents had all the necessary genes to account for the . . . necessary genetic markers . . . The explanation had to be that the woman was actually two people in one: Two eggs must have begun development as fraternal twins but then merged into one, each contributing some tissues to the single embryo."

Ever since then, I've given James the benefit of whatever doubts I still entertain. And from here on, I'm glad to let him speak for himself.

—Tam Mossman
July 14, 1992

PART ONE

Where

You

Are

Now

1

The Channeling *Im*plosion—
You Are Part of
Whatever You Contact

• Who James claims to be • His definition of channeling and motive for answering questions • How entities communicate via the channeling process • The three levels of channeling • The subconscious as natural mimic: why "possession" and channeling are essentially the same • How trance personalities assemble a persona from characteristics already in the medium's subconscious • The wisdom of taking trance personalities with a grain of salt

James, who exactly are you? The spirit of a deceased person?

"The spirit *of* one deceased" seems to imply that the individual is diminished at death, and that only a scanty portion of one's original being remains. Now, if you ask questions of something *less* than 100 percent of its previous total, what kind of answers do you expect to get back?

There are indeed mediums who channel the personalities of ones recently deceased. I, however, am better described as a gestalt, a self-aware linking-up of what would—to you—seem a multitude of separate, conscious individuals . . . a goodly number of whom are alive and well in your present world.

Your computers increase in strength and ability as they have access to more electrical relays. So it is with conscious identity: although my "components" are able to exist independently, when linked up on my non-physical level, they are able to coalesce into yet another, higher level of consciousness that I identify as "me." This is not too far-fetched, if you consider that you yourself are composed of several trillion cells that live and die without your being aware of it. Your waking consciousness is a byproduct of their activity.

Can you explain what channeling is and how it works?

Your world has hardly agreed what channeling truly is, so it would seem I am compounding the confusion by telling you what channeling is *not*. But by doing so, I expect to clear away some of the misconceptions that prevent you from seeing this hardly uncommon art form for what it really is.

Our friend Tam is now letting his mind wander, picking up words from me in short bursts or clusters and taking them down on a typewriter, with no real concern for speed nor accuracy. He is listening—with more than the physical ears, of course—for these words to emerge, chosen from among the words and concepts already in his memory. From his peaceful example, you can see that channeling is not some dramatic battle for the poor mortal nervous system. Nor does it distort the incarnate end of the partnership in any way.

Rather, channeling at its best—in the refined form that I and many of my colleagues are endeavoring to promote among you—can be compared to what happens when your brain sends a signal to your fingers to type. Mute though your fingers be, yet they can spell words on a keyboard. And "unspiritual" though your unconscious is said to be, yet it can transmit concepts of a most divine nature.

Just as the violin transmits and amplifies sound, so does a channeler transmit and amplify the "signal" coming from one such as I. Such transmissions would not be possible unless both source and transmitter were of the same essential substance, able to resonate in tune with one another. And if you step back and view the typing typist, you will agree that brain, fingers, and intervening nerves are all one single entity—one being.

In ways most difficult to describe, you are helping to create my words even as you sit reading them, long after they were taken down. Never believe that such "miracles" as channeling are performed only by a few! Simply by reading, you too have become a channeler of sorts, taking into your mind words that, as far as you are concerned, never existed before you opened this book—words that can now resonate and speak to other layers of your being. Yet this is nothing new or strange, for channeling happens 24 hours a day *to each and every one of you*, whether you know it or not! Every one of you constantly receives and alters the greater energies that sustain you, even as air pressure sustains the balloon, as momentum sustains the arc of the waterfall.

You have had millions of years of practice, and I am speaking to you both as a species and as individuals. Your mental and physical "shape" is produced by a constant channeling. Your loves, desires, greatest joys, and deepest terrors are all real-life distillations of greater realities which you, as adroit channels, have "picked up" from dimensions imperceptible to your five senses. You are constantly translating—or channeling—the sunrise, the new moon in the western sky, the chirrup of birds and night breezes into impressions that your senses can perceive. For if you did not translate them with your nervous system, how could they present themselves to your perception?

I assure you that not all communication exists in words such as you are pondering now. Your very lives have their own nouns and verbs, their own nuances of greater meaning—which comprise the greater "sentences" and "paragraphs" that you know as nations, or as centuries. You are letters and punctuation upon the Page of Life, set down by a loving Hand that expresses itself most eloquently. And thus, each of you is a "message"—*in physical, living terms*—from an invisible "beyond" that seems mysterious only because it lies within you, intimately, where your rational mind cannot turn to glimpse it.

As a simple mortal, I've been judging discarnate entities. Sometimes I think there's a world championship going on among them. Which trance personality is best for me to listen to?

I would remind you that there is no such thing—on your Earth or elsewhere—as a *simple* mortal. Human beings are never simple in any way!

Now, there is indeed a World Olympics of Channeling going on in the *minds* of many of you. Every day, and every night in your dream state, you hold your own personal Olympics. In those trials and decathlons of your own minds, you weigh the "truths," the opinions, the slants and particular attitudes that you have read and encountered, constantly weighing one hero against another. What if Seattle Slew had run against Dan Patch? You compare Plato to Kant, sometimes to Jack Kerouac or Allen

Ginsberg! Yes, there is a championship going on, and yet you individuals hold the timers.

For many of you, the New Testament is champ. For others of you, the *Bhagavad-Gita* or the Old Testament holds the current heavyweight title. For still others of you, the first five Books of the Bible or the Upanishads are swiftest and Best in Show. My humble words are indeed breathing down the stretch, but there would be no joy in sports if the winner were predetermined. If you had only your heavyweight title-holder alone in the ring, with no contenders competing merely for the fun of competition, that would be a rather sorry sports event.

So I encourage you to award the prize to those who move the quickest in *your* imagination. I will be happy to enter that kind of contest, but only if you also admit to competition as many other moral authorities as you can—for the more entities you pit me against, the richer will your personal Olympics be.

If I am defeated by a greater wit or a greater philosopher, tremendous—then you are the true winner! As long as I can stay here in the ring, bloody but unbowed, the longer you are going to seek *more* interesting old spooks to listen to, and the more goodies you are going to pick up along the way. When finally those Olympics come to a close, you will be the one who carries home the bronze and the silver and the gold; and not I.

If the after-death state is so pleasant, why have you come here to speak with us this afternoon?

For the same reason you have come to listen: Basically, because I enjoy it.

You have individuals who like to go camping—that is their idea of a vacation. But when you are sitting in your penthouse, with champagne in your glass and a symphony on the stereo, you may wonder how anyone could *enjoy* going out with the bears and midges and tsetse flies, to sleep under the cold stars with several rocks in the wrong places, and cook greasy bacon in the morning—while you are breakfasting on croissants and Colombian coffee.

How can this be? Of course, the campers are seeking a different kind of amusement.

When I speak to you now, it is quite like incarnating. When *you* incarnated, however, it was as if you took a belly flop off the high dive: Once you leave your "diving board" to enter an infant body, you cannot return quite as easily—it is usually a one-way trip, and you have to swim to the other end of the pool. You might say I am just putting my foot into the water to communicate with you, my colleagues—who are in the swim of it, as it were.

There are always people strengthening their muscles, learn-ing new crawls and backstrokes, by being in the swim of physical existence. After their workout, it feels wonderful to shower, towel off, have a martini up on deck, and watch everyone else thrashing around in the pool. Yet unless they had a good workout, they would not enjoy the relaxation. And—trust me!—after a certain amount of relaxation, you will feel restless and want to get back in the pool. There are other Olympic-size pools, besides this Earth, in which you can get your feet wet.

Why are all you entities communicating with us? Do you have something to accomplish?

Yes, indeed! You know that if you are loving parents, you teach your children proper manners. Now, basically I am teaching you—or reminding you, rather—of the way things are done when you become "adult" in *my* terms.

You teach children manners because you do not want to be surrounded by a group of louts in twenty years' time, so I am taking a bit of my "time" to assure myself that you will know your p's and q's when you wind up on my side of the fence. My mission is not to tell you that I come from the Other Side, but rather, to affirm that we are all on the *same* side here!

I know it can be tedious to be a child—I've been a child many times—because adults are always telling you what to do. But if they weren't, you would quickly forget all of their wonderful lessons. You adults have different concerns than a child might have—and rightly so!—but so has a child equal right to different concerns than the adult. Yet child and adult are still the same species. And the differences between *our* separate realities and points of view in no way pre-suppose that you and I are alien or unconnected to one another. Rather, those differences merely represent stages of growth—*necessary* stages of growth. You are in no way inferior for not having the abilities I possess, any more than you could blame yourself at age 12 for not having the strength or intellect that you will have at age 24.

It would be absurd to judge yourself by the same standards. But, it would be a serious error not to aspire to the accomplishments of the next higher stage: "If I am now 30 years old, I know what I would like to be when I am 40. If I am now 40, I know what I would like to be at 50. If I am now incarnate, I know what I would like to be between lives . . . "

Do you enjoy satisfying our curiosity?

Far be it from me to satisfy anyone's curiosity! To do so would be like chloroforming a butterfly or pressing a flower in a book where it could grow no more.

I will try to answer your questions. But as for satisfying your curiosities, I would never attempt such a horrendous violation of your source of joy and creativity!

Why do you discarnate entities seem eager to answer certain questions, while passing over others?

It may interest you that I perceive your questions in much the same way as you would perceive a triangle, cube, or cylinder—that is, primarily as a geometric shape and not merely as to what that shape "represents" by its symbolism or its contents.

An idle question—one seeking only to scratch the surface-itch of curiosity—I perceive as a two-dimensional figure without depth, and seldom with interesting color or texture. Yet a question arising from real need, *that* I perceive as a three-dimensional funnel or whirlpool sending out its own particular form of "gravity," to which I am by nature attracted. In a sense, I do not provide the answer as much as I *become* the answer, so that your questions set me challenges of greater or lesser appeal.

I hasten to interject that my analogies as to shape and color are just that—analogies. Obviously, I do not "see" a given question as a pink rhomboid, but I do sense questions on a non-verbal basis. My answers, too—at least, before Tam's subconscious translates them—are provided in non-verbal form. Later, I will endeavor to explain exactly how a human mind translates these symbols of mine—or of *ours*, actually—into words and, moreover, constructs the kind of "personality" you may perceive as discarnate.

In short, you need not voice a question to have it answered. You may, of course, write it down and share with others the beauty of its symmetry and special colors—warm (or attractive) or cool (or threatening). But the very presence of sincere curiosity within you will inevitably prompt answers from your surrounding world, non-verbal though these answers may be. And each answer will be repeated endlessly until your question takes it in, feeds upon it, and thereby transmutes itself into curiosity of a higher order.

For curiosity—perhaps more obviously from my point of view than yours—is never satisfied, never completed. Rather, questions and their answers grow in tandem, like the footprints of a graceful dancer, or like a crystal that organizes similar matter in its nearby vicinity, only to grow larger and exert a more powerful organizing force. Some questions are basically statements with hooks at the end, half-statements designed to complete themselves. And like many species of animals, questions are highly choosy and will not content themselves with just any answer: The sloppy question that can be answered carelessly is no true question at all.

I am not denying it is valuable to write questions down. Such an exercise helps precise-ify the thought behind the question, helps rehearse the underlying emotions and, perhaps most important of all, exteriorizes the question and gives it additional energy—a spin of extra momentum that may help it on its quest. But when you read answers such as are given on the pages that follow, it is best to read each one several times, with perhaps a day or two between readings. A good answer, just like a good source of nourishment, will attract poor, starving, underfed questions from all areas of your psyche. They will feed upon this splendid new answer, grow strong, and send up a caterwauling to be acknowledged and to be fed new answers all their own.

Thus, strongest answers nourish new questions, and strongest questions nourish new answers; in a giddy and exhilarating spiral—as it should be. So try to take the same delight in forming questions as I do in forming answers— for indeed, you provide "answers" each time you water a plant, cook dinner for a child, breathe air into a stuffy room, or feed a beloved cat who is rubbing at your ankles. Questions are a means of seeking what is needed; and answers a form of nourishment that can *sustain* curiosity but never lay it to rest—any more than you can expect this morning's hearty breakfast to tide you over the next 40 years.

There is a certain trap in asking questions, however. Like a hunter who wastes many arrows to fell a single prey, you may find yourselves penning page after page of questions. But after some reflection, you will see that they all point at a single answer. This is why I will often not reply to precisely the question you asked, or may answer only one car out of an entire railroad train of curiosity, or may even give you an answer that seems irrelevant—my way of telling you that your quarry must not be sought where you expected to find it.

Rest assured that you do have the answer you need, and that any answer good enough to satisfy one question will usually provide enough leftovers to feed the rest of the litter.

I'm curious as to how you picked this particular individual to channel yourself through.

Part of your question is, "What does one do to get picked?"

First off, our friend Tam has always had an attitude of "I'll try anything once. If it's nice, I'll try it again"—to put it rather delicately. He has an open mind, a rich imagination, and a mild contempt for received wisdom. Such individuals make good channels because they are not going to put us on Cloud Nine, graft wings upon our shoulders or halos upon our heads. They are going to accept our ideas, even when our suggestions rather seriously contradict their own belief systems.

In this case, I more or less took charge, communicated with our friend here, and got his tacit permission to try out a trance. During the period when his consciousness "collapsed in upon itself"—the best way I could describe it to you—I stroked his consciousness as if it were a kitten sleeping in my lap, making it feel warm and secure and protected.

We've had no trouble since, for he lets me say whatever comes into his head. From his point of view, therefore, I can make a fool of myself—though of course I do not! But were I to do so, it would not be him at whom you threw the bricks and shot the arrows. We are divorced, in that sense, though ours is a very tight marriage: We are separate, equal, but by no means interchangeable.

Can you elaborate on the actual mechanics of channeling?
How do your thoughts come to be spoken by a medium? Why
are some trance personalities much more reliable than others?

It may be of service to think of the human subconscious as
the tympanum, or eardrum, of the psyche as a whole.

"Outside" the tympanum is a world—not of sound, but of air-
borne vibrations. These vibrations are transmitted by the eardrum
and hammer, anvil, and stirrup of the inner ear, picked up by nerve
sensors and carried ultimately to the brain, and consciousness.
"Out there," a Beethoven symphony can be charted as a series of
high and low peaks on a graph. "In here," within the brain, is where
the music attains its true beauty. Yet just as a music student will
perceive sweeter, more delightful touches than will a musical ig-
noramus listening to the same recording, so can an enlightened,
educated channel "hear" more of what we have to communicate.

Let me say, again by way of analogy, that consciously perceived sound can arise from *within* the ear as well as from without. Ringing in the ears, for example, can arise from a disorder in
the middle ear. So with much of what arises from the Quija board:
Certain elements within the psyche, when called upon to transmit
"sounds" from outside, feel inadequate if they have no such sounds
to transmit. And even though they are well within the confines of
the psyche, they assume the roles of outside spirits.

It's as if the hammer, anvil, and stirrup realized that no
symphony was playing "outside" the membrane of the self.
But because the conscious mind was avidly requesting some
music, these tiny bones thought they might as well strike up a
little ditty of their own. All too often, these inner components
of the psyche are making such joyous, if chaotic, noise that
when such as we come to whisper, our preliminary words
are garbled, if they can be transmitted at all.

I should add, in parentheses, that almost all elements of the
psyche are programmed to grow to independence if given half a
chance. This truth is behind your myth of the brooms that grew from
splinters in "The Sorcerer's Apprentice," and the creatures
in the movie *Gremlins*. Just as your body is composed of more or
less autonomous cells, so is any psyche a vast colony of individual
impulses, any of which can easily awaken itself to independent
life. In most instances, a disruptive—or overly independent—

psyche fragment is allowed to bud off into other realities, just as convicts and miscreants in 18th-century England were allowed free passage to Botany Bay on the other side of the world. But had the rogues been allowed to remain in England—and if a self-awakened portion of the subconscious is allowed to stay "within" the psyche—then rebellion and contention could arise.

I hope this digression makes my main point even clearer. You might say the first level of "discarnate" transmission arises from safely within the psyche. Many spirits who act as if they should know better are not external at all, but simply newborn (and thus, rather childish and overeager-to-please) splinters of the mind. To be rid of their obsessive chatter and fearful whining, you need only give them permission to depart—that, and the assurance that they will grow to better health and greater pleasures than are possible in their current confined state. (A myth that states this rather clearly is that of Athena springing full-grown from the forehead of Zeus.)

Such interior imps, not yet ready for—or yet allowed—a full and independent existence, comprise the first level of communicating "spirits."

The second level of discarnate intelligence *is* external to the psyche. Imagine, again as analogy, a parrot who sits on one's shoulder, whispering words into one's ear. This source is external, but on a co-equal level with the one who receives its messages. A dear relative, or one who has passed beyond death with a great longing for earthly existence—often of social orientation—may desire to come through still-incarnates, much as a high school athlete, fearful of the challenges of college, might hang around the football field to visit those who used to cheer him when he played on the varsity team.

These entities form the ranks of what used to be called spirit guides. But because their main motive is to communicate with the living, they do not venture very far afield in search of answers. Like the parrot, they stay close by those they speak to, seldom spreading their wings. Again, a myth: Because Noah's dove flew *far* out over the waters, she returned not with mere words, but with a symbol of fecundity and harvest.

After death, it is in the nature of an entity to partly dismantle itself, to swell and grow even as an insect that has shed its skin is ready to become larger and more resplendent than before. An unhealthy attachment to earthly communications can, in a sense, deform a new-dead spirit. Like a parrot with clipped wings, reluctant to venture beyond the comforting shoulders of those who love to hear it speak, the newly dead will seldom reach beyond themselves to report of new realities that might disturb their old friends: They will quite literally parrot familiar truths still held on Earth. Yes, spirit guides may see ahead, and accurately, but not necessarily see much farther or much better than could an incarnate's own inner senses.

The third level, of course, is the one from which I speak to you. I am the sum total of a number of entities of whom Tam is one. You might say I find myself downstream of Tam: His experiences, achievements, understandings all flow not *down* but *into* me, along with input from a wide variety of other entities and forms of consciousness. Just as waves and ripples can travel upriver, so can I send vibrations back to my component parts, as you might flex your cramped toes or, out of compassion as well as self-interest, gently warm the fingers that have numbed themselves while doing your bidding.

In another sense—for I do not want this river analogy to be taken too literally, lest I be compared to a Sargasso Sea or a "Dead" Sea or one who runs on at the mouth—I am a "later" Tam. Tam is an embryonic me. And, as you can easily understand, I take good care of my early versions. Their "continued" health greatly increases my own well-being and range of abilities.

I can communicate *directly* only with those in your world who are "upstream" of me. I *could* communicate with others who are not a part of me, but only by resonance. That is, I would have to communicate with their larger entity—with one of my own equals, on the level at which I find myself—and ask that my message be passed along. Because of the great tact and accuracy on our level (an outgrowth and development of the honesty quite prevalent on yours), such a message would be delivered in quite the same form that I transmitted it. But you should never mistake the mailman for the one who has written the letter.

Exactly how do you communicate with us, then? By possessing the medium?

I am not possessing our friend here. Rather, his unconscious mind patiently waits to receive images and vibrations and then passes them along to consciousness.

I, at my end, operate much as do your talking horses. I move through the channel's vocabulary-memory, patiently pointing out those concepts and word-associations I wish to convey. Then the channel's subconscious faculties translate my impulses into an assemblage of consecutive words. Occasionally in these communications, the syntax slips. Tam registers dissatisfaction. And so, I "precise-ify" my thoughts, and Tam's subconscious obliges by restating my words for me.

Tourists in a foreign country often overhear snatches of native tongues which they interpret as English. Similarly, young parents can be convinced their baby's liquid gurgles are actually "Daddy"—because the ear-brain system, having built up certain quantum units of sound and meaning, finds it simplest to interpret *all* sounds of a certain nature as "Daddy." So it is with your unconscious: To get my message through, I must choose symbols and ideas that I know Tam's abilities will transmit accurately.

Even your best mediums occasionally depart into wild fantasy —the result of the unconscious being slipped some concept for which it is wholly unprepared, and can translate only as gibberish. If you have no experience of the rhinoceros, you will channel tales of unicorns. If you have no concept of the kind of peaceable brotherhood in which I reside, you might tell tall tales of Atlantis—which sank out of sight and thus represents the hidden wellspring of knowledge and wisdom that you all sense within yourselves. Not that Atlantis never was, but you have buried it more deeply under myths and allegories than Nature ever buried it beneath the waves.

Tam's subconscious even lends me a certain persona—the characteristics of a still-human personality. Similarly, civilized visitors to a rural tribe are, by way of compliment, offered the chance to garb themselves in native dress. When I first came through Tam, I took on the characteristics I did simply because that was how he expected a visitor from outside his psyche to behave. It is only tactful to obey the customs of your host and not to assert your own individuality at the expense of others.

Not that I am beguiling or deceiving anyone by withholding my true essence. To put it simply, Tam's unconscious can express some of my characteristics more easily than others—and these happen to be the characteristics most likely to "pass" in human society. How I appear in these communications is, in a real sense, shaped and determined by *your* ideas of what a trance personality should be.

To transmit information accurately, your unconscious mind must be at least as versatile as the human middle ear, which can "mimic" all kinds of sounds from without and transmit them accurately. Thus when you read my words, recall that they are a translation provided by Tam's unconscious. His Level-One "gremlins" have gone their way, for their own development, and he conveniently abandoned the idea of keeping a recently-dead budgie on his psychic shoulder. Instead, he let his inner channels open up so that I consciously might share with him at least part of the huge amount he unknowingly shares with me.

Does possession as depicted in The Exorcist *really occur? What allows it to happen? And what do you recommend to prevent it?*

Possession *as depicted* in that movie does in fact occur. But the real cause is not the devil or outside entities, as you may have been led to believe, and the preventive treatment is not primarily religious in nature.

In many non-technological societies, simple illness—"simple" according to your present-day definition—is seen as the work of evil spirits. The swelling of an infection, fever, depression, and mental illnesses are all seen as afflictions alien to the sufferer, arising from one sort of possession or another.

And *in essence*, such an interpretation is strictly accurate, because illness, of whatever variety, is a product of unbalanced development of the host personality. One part of the body, or one of its systems, seeks to grow—or *not* grow—at another's expense. As a result, the organism is weakened in specific areas, literally inviting a specific disease—whether manifested by the body's own cells or by the sudden unrestrained growth of a virus or bacterium. In short, the physical illness is allowed to manifest a repressed or "minority" thought in fleshy form. But the same impulses and energy could be more healthily manifested through coherent, balanced change and outward action.

As with physical illness, so with imbalances of the mind —for after all, the latter cause the former! Certain metabolic diseases, including the one manifested most commonly as warts, result in bizarre growths that seem relatively independent of the body on which they occur.

But hasn't it been proven that warts are caused by a virus?

Indeed it has. But what do you suppose activates the virus in the first place? I suggest the basic cause of warts is a meta-bolic disorder that lets small deposits of unexcreted substance lodge in the skin—small, but sufficient to act as a catalyst or "fertilizer" for viral particles. It is a disorder similar to, but infinitely less severe than, gout. A test of the blood of wart sufferers will someday reveal its presence.

Now, a wart assumes more or less the same shape, regardless of the body part on which it occurs; even though its component cells are, in fact, those of the body. With that preamble in mind, you are in a better position to comprehend so-called possession.

As I said, the psyche is constantly budding off and seeding new parts of itself, joyously and adventurously, into new realities, *including*—and this is important to remember—*into its own perceived present.* The mind's main focus is forward, into the im-mediate future it has selected for itself, just as an animal racing across the ground is most attentive to the turf directly before it.

If the immediate future appears blocked—not dangerous, because danger is usually perceived as challenge on the deepest level of the psyche—but *blocked*, then the psyche endeavors to flow around the present obstacle, much as an amoeba would attempt to do. And if the psyche produces too many "arms," it can, in a sense, lose track of them. Multi-focus consciousness is natural and easy at the Oversoul level, but it is not always possible for a single human psyche—much less a relatively child-ish, immature one—to hold its various extensions in simultaneous focus. Thus, you get cases of split personality as well as posses-sion. In the former instances, semi-independent personalities manifest themselves as human, as in the case of Sybil. In the lat-ter, they take on the guise of demons, as depicted in *The Exorcist.*

I invite you to view the parallels and similarities. Your experts agree that clinical split personality is almost always sparked by the core personality having suffered child abuse at a young age. Similarly, possession often afflicts the young and supposedly innocent—children, women, would-be saints, and others who have considered themselves "molested" by a hostile, or at best in-different, universe. If the hostility of a parent can snap a young mind into defensive fragments that seek to scurry and hide, how much more of a fragmenting blow can be dealt by the horrendous concept of a malevolent universe—or a Hell that seeks to punish transient sins with punishment everlasting? The more you believe in torments reserved for the damned, the more you must believe in the depths of evil that would merit such a fate.

Recall that in practically every case of possession, the devils or demons act subhuman or, at best, less than adult. They swear, make noises, play pranks, and hardly comport themselves as what they are alleged to be—fallen angels, higher than Man in the order of creation. I can assure you that no self-aware discarnate of my level ever debases itself! Any entity manifesting such coarse selfishness and vulgarity is on its way *up*, not down.

Now, every so often, the exorcising priest meets up with a Lucifer or Beelzebub who carries himself with dignity and speaks fine Latin, and any number of languages. But so it is with split personalities—usually there is a core entity, wiser and more mature than the rest, who acts as the ringleader and manifests admirable abilities that, essentially, compensate for the feeling of powerlessness experienced by the originating psyche.

Another parallel your parapsychologists have overlooked is that possession is often associated with poltergeist activity. Is it not conceivable, then, that the "demons" are merely poltergeists manifesting within the body and nervous system—just as a virus, unimpeded, swiftly takes on a life of its own within the tissues? I remind you that the youthful fragments of the psyche are natural chameleons, innate actors. To insure their survival, they do not just blend in with their surroundings, but assume the appearance and behavior of more highly developed entities —ideally, coming across as authority figures with whom you would not care to mess. And so, the most junior of your psychic fragments (and everyone, healthy or not, has them to one degree or another) will typically announce themselves through the Ouija board as Alexander the Great or Louis XIV. Or, through the entranced mouth of a troubled youngster, they may style themselves the Hound of Hell, Ashtoreth, or Moloch—and take understandable delight in the alacrity with which they are believed.

One further fact that your professionals have failed to notice: A "possessing spirit" usually obeys, *and very strictly indeed*, the tenets of whatever religious creed its core personality was brought up in. Thus, you have Buddhist demons, Catholic demons, Protestant Episcopalian demons, even Hindu and Shinto demons—each of which is sent fleeing by a ritual of the appropriate sect. Now, if you suppose that each subspecies of demon must be quelled by a different religious antibiotic, you are postulating a most complex universe indeed!

I would suggest a simpler explanation, by way of an observation self-evident to any minister: Pure, unswerving, unquestioning faith in organized religion is most prevalent in those who *perceive* themselves as powerless. Is it a coincidence that these candidates for orthodoxy are often the "victims" of entities who obey their religious world-view right down to the letter? Such following-the-dots with consistency and precision is one of the typical ways in which an insecure being seeks approval and a sense of identity.

With these theorems in mind, I believe you can work out the remainder of the equation for yourself.

If you Third-Level trance personalities are psychologically independent of your channels, why do you use some of Tam's verbal mannerisms, as well as examples from his personal experience?

It would be stranger still if I did not do so at all! Just as Picasso—to borrow an example familiar to the man through whom I speak—constructed the sculpture of a baboon out of two toy cars, so such as I can do things with pre-formed words and ideas that their original maker never intended.

Theoretically, it would be possible to create whole new images; new words, even. But if I can express my essence and creativity through Tam's rather rich assortment of memories, why not? It makes things easier! To a large extent, coming through a mortal is, for us, a kind of play: Just as you might enjoy crawling around on the rug with a beloved infant, so I enjoy returning and being able to manipulate the verbal symbols and brain-based associations that are as dearly alien to me as blocks and a rattle might be to you.

I have now encountered Seth, Ramtha, Lazaris, and John, whom I heard at the Seth Conference in Austin—

You have a very full dance card, it seems!

—and my question to you *is, why do you guys all manifest an accent from the British Isles or thereabouts?*

You might as well ask, "Where did you get that lovely tie?" or "Why do you come dressed in that particular outfit?"

So-called trance personalities, such as I modestly claim to be, often speak with strange accents. Mine own has been variously termed "definitely Welsh," Indian, English, Scottish, and American Indian. The real question is, where do we get our personae?

In many of your legends, a mortal asks to see a discarnate in all of his, her, or its glory—and is somewhat worse the wear as a result of that encounter. To be comprehensible to you, we must use your conventions and ways of doing things: "When in Rome, do as the Romans do." Thus, when we come to channel ourselves through a cooperative individual, we dress up! We rummage through the unconscious imagery of one such as our friend here, and select a "costume" to make us visible to you. We might say, "Well, we don't want to be *too* disreputable, so we shall not speak in monosyllables or use terribly bad grammar." No four-letter words, unless they happen to be ones like *love* or *hope*, you see!

I quite consciously adopt a persona. So did Seth—he admitted it. Almost every so-called entity has his own gestures and accents, drawn from the attics and steamer trunks of the unconscious of the individual through whom he speaks.

Therefore, if you hear the words of a single entity through several channels, you can of course expect differences. Not everyone has jackets in the same size, so when I speak through others—yes, I do, but not under the name of James —I will not necessarily use this accent, or even one like it. I must wear whatever happens to be on *their* rack. It is difficult, therefore, for you to try to track us down from channel to channel, even as it would be foolish to seek only

Rocky Mountain breezes and assume that the winds blowing in the Adirondacks are somehow lacking, for they do not whistle through the pines in quite the same way.

You all have many voices, besides mine, which can teach you. So do not listen merely to one of us, but rejoice that you have so many to which you can listen.

We *could* speak to you in the wind, in the joy of your own breath, in a glimpse of sunlight on a river, or in a soaring bird's wings—and, of course, we do. But when we so communicate, you do not say, "Seth, John, James, thank you so much!" You say, "Oh, just a bird," or "Oh, only a river!" Nor do you thank *yourselves* for being able to perceive that beauty around you—which you ascribe to the outside only.

Wouldn't we find it healthier to think things out for ourselves, rather than risk delusion by believing in you or in some other teacher?

Yes, and you are already doing that! When you come to me for answers, you are likely to go home laden with even more questions. That is my way—sneakily, I admit!—of getting you to think for yourselves, do your own private investigations into your personal universes, and lay down rules that apply to your individual turf and none other. How else, but via your beliefs and your biases, can you show forth your individuality?

You are always risking enlightenment, even as you risk delusion. But delusion is never permanent, while enlightenment is—or at least, it boosts you up to a level where you can risk a better class of delusion!

I do not mind in the least if you do not believe in me. I would definitely take offense, however, if you refuse to believe in yourself.

2

Early Man and His Divine Mistakes

• Limits of James's knowledge • The origins of duality • Purpose and symbolism of Peru's Nazca Lines • Pre-Columbian aircraft? • Prehistoric surveying: how an ice-free Antarctica was mapped • Atlantean technology • Roots of the unicorn legend • How ancient wisdom is rediscovered • Aztec human sacrifice and modern life insurance • The source of cruelty • Some words on Mary Magdalene and how the New Testament was composed • Satanism and the distortions of organized religions • Did Francis Bacon write Hamlet? *• Historical events as analogies of present experience—and why aspects of the past* must *remain vague • The virtues of error*

If you are all-knowing and doing your best to educate us, could you start from the very beginning, as the Bible does?

I am hardly all-knowing! In fact, my limitations allow me to make contact with you at all. Were I the vast reservoir of knowledge that you presuppose me to be, I could no more fit myself through Tam's subconscious than could your proverbial rope enter through the eye of a needle.

True, I can perceive present and future probabilities, but only somewhat more clearly than you yourselves are able to do, on an unconscious level. Also, through various of my "past" incarnations, I am intimately acquainted with certain discrete time periods in your historical past—and future. But because I am not composed of *all* the personalities that have ever lived on Earth, my view of history is still somewhat limited—spotty, in fact, for my own inclinations have led me to incarnate in certain areas and periods in preference over others.

If you ask me about medieval Japan or pre-Columbian Latin America, you are not likely to be disappointed. I found those eras extremely advantageous to my overall development, and in fact managed to incarnate myself as an entire tribe, generation after generation, in what you now call Ecuador. But there are other time periods—such as when the Pyramids were under construction, when your first colonists land on Mars—when I have been absent or, rather, when my attention was or will be elsewhere. I would not burden you with the confused hearsay I picked up second-hand, as it were, in lives adjacent to those periods. There is enough guesswork going on at an incarnate level, and I hardly wish to add to that sorry jumble.

It is possible for me to incarnate "backward" into a given probable past; though of course *all* times, even your present, are probable—which makes incarnation possible in the first place. Thus, if I take a "refresher course" or life in your so-called past, I may well be able to answer a question that presently lies outside my grasp. But my development in this regard is hard to correlate with your conception of linear "time." To you, my expansions and incarnations would appear spasmodic, as sudden and apparently impulsive as the lunge of a frog for an insect. For this reason, I can't ask you to be patient. It does not take *time* to incarnate, but does require a more precise *confluence of opportunity*—a distinction you can probably remember on your own, if you think back in calm and quiet to your last "time" between lives.

I would rather answer your questions about the "past" from first-hand knowledge, or not at all; for lacking memories that are relatively uncontaminated, I must deal with a past more or less fabricated from perceptions and preconceptions of others who have lived through—or meditated upon—that period. This is not unlike trying to decipher a mosaic paved over and painted with white lines for use as a parking lot! Certain eras of your time, such as the fall of Atlantis and the days of Jesus, have been so overlaid and retouched with imaginative speculation that their "original" truth can hardly be perceived by an outsider who was not there.

To give an idea of the complexity of things, there are separate Christs for every one of your Protestant and Catholic sects, plus some Jesuses who traversed India or the Americas, others who came from space, still others who remained there. And to the degree that any imaginative creation takes on a life of its own, all of these probable Christs are, in a very real sense, valid and "historical."

Your present world is a most charming flower arrangement, culled from different pasts—many of which were mutually exclusive. Just as "present" flowers from separate "past" bulbs can be aligned in a single vase, so can the logical consequences of different probabilities come together without *too* much contradiction. You have allowed the offspring of these contradictory pre-worlds to lie down together without incident, for your species required broader stimulation than any one of them could have provided by itself.

In another answer, I will talk about the binary star system that your world "once" had the choice of being part of, and of the numerous satellites that used to ring your firmament before the arrival of your present moon. These pasts are as unsubstantial and unprovable as yesterday, because they are equally irretrievable. And because these pasts *are* safely past, as you think of them, your current world can allow their contradictory fruits to persist. Only your astronomers and scientists, capable of seeing deeply into the physical gridlock of existence, are baffled by a Nature who seems intent on contradicting her own rules. But if She made those rules in the first place, surely She has the right to break them!

Someday I will tell you my version of the Creation Myth as I recall and experienced that sequence—or rather, gathering—of events, with the enormous qualification that this "past beginning" is every bit as illusory as the ones that each of you creates for yourself. Each man stands on his own feet, on a separate area of soil. And while your personal pasts are interconnected and recognizably the same "body" of experience, you each stand on and arise from a microcosm uniquely your own. The pebble under your toe is like no pebble trod upon by your brother. So forgive me if I do not get bogged down in discussing all those individual pebbles, but only the overall geologic substrata of the past upon which you *all* stand—and can substantially agree.

How and why did the concept of duality arise? Is it associated with this reality system only?

Duality is less of a *concept*, in your terms, than a mental filing system—a means of categorizing information based, in turn, on your biological predisposition toward bilateral symmetry.

Your world falls neatly and conveniently into opposites—light and dark, up and down, right and left—but these dichotomies are simply the results of being corporeal. A creature without sight will hardly distinguish light and dark. You, having two arms and legs, naturally have a firm sense of left and right. But with other creatures of different configuration—a starfish or paramecium, say—such easy divisions would by no means be possible. The starfish, in effect, experiences the world from all sides, as does the jellyfish; as do most plants. For them, any experience is one point along a spectrum, or a specific tuning on a broader dial.

On worlds where the sun is obscured by a heavy cloud cover, or where the planet is illumined by a series of satellites or by a binary star system, concepts of duality are naturally "fuzzier" than on Earth. Earlier in your planet's history, a number of satellites were in orbit around the then-equator, so that the night was very well lit. Gravity was lighter. Your current moon joined the Earth at a far later date, and its arrival caused the plummeting of the other, more inward satellites. Scars of their falling still exist in the crust of your world, and their downfall was responsible for the extinguishing of a number of species, in a winter that was not nuclear but, you might say, lunar.

The point of this digression is that many of your still-present species evolved on a world where light was relatively constant, where the only "duality" was the basic one of up and down, imposed by gravity. In yet another probable solar system very closely related to your own, one of the outer gas giants— Saturn, I believe—became a small dwarf star. Some of the probable creatures that evolved on this warmer, brighter planet of yours are present with you now—again, the starfish, and many plants whose leaves branch in all directions, like a bromeliad's. Accustomed to light from a wider angle, they had no need to lean, as do your branching trees and stemmed plants. A high, heavy cloud cover and thinner atmosphere kept things from overheating, as a great deal of energy was reflected back into space.

Duality, then, is a concept rooted deeply in your genes and in the fabric of your physical being. But just as your old-brain system is not the most reliable guide to conduct in a civilized world, neither is duality the best all-around concept with which to partition and evaluate your daily experience. You need, as individuals and as a race, to open your minds to a broader constellation of possibilities. Ideas that *necessarily* contradict one another only serve to cram the wide range of your experience into two mutually exclusive filing cabinets.

Peru's enormous Nazca Lines cannot be seen from the ground. Were they constructed as navigational guides or landing strips?

Your question presupposes that only from an aircraft or a hovering balloon can one observe configurations on the ground.

The natives in the Nazca region had a rather extensive background in the art of astral projection. In large measure, the Nazca images served as a kind of enormous final exam to be taken, almost inadvertently, by those being trained to project. Only when out of their bodies would trainees report those strange, exotic figures in the earth to the west of the tribe's main dwelling area; and the teachers would know that their pupils had succeeded.

Basically, though, the Lines, like some modern-day hex signs, were constructed to ward off malicious spirits—specifically meteorites, of which the Nazca were especially fearful, having seen some real beauties come flaming down to explode large craters in the earth. Thus in part, the Nazca Lines were the exact *opposite* of a landing strip. Their intended meaning was, "Don't land here!" That same message was extended to tribes on the other side of the mountains, whom the Nazca assumed to be equally adept in projection as themselves.

It is well to remember that secular art—or pure illusionistic representation—evolved only recently in your Western culture, during the Renaissance. Everywhere else, art either has a deeper spiritual meaning or else is considered worse than scribbles.

In Central America, archaeologists have unearthed little gold objects that resemble jet planes. According to at least one aeronautical engineer, planes built according to these models could actually fly. Did the ancients have airplanes?

Yes and no. They had *toys*—small craft that children could launch into the air and fly for short distances. Any people, no matter how technologically indifferent, could observe a soaring butterfly or bird and be prompted to craft a small replica that, after a certain amount of trial and error, would fly.

Look upon today's charm bracelets, and you will find humorous or otherwise frivolous objects sculpted of precious metal. So it was with the ancients of Central America, but their soaring toys carried a religious meaning as well. Sail-planes came to be taken

as symbols for the human soul, which can soar even while
the body remains grounded. Since a small palm-leaf toy would
fly while a heavier one made of lumber would not, they
also served as a proverbial admonition to "travel light," physically
and in terms of moral debts and emotional entanglements.

Thus, a sail-plane cast in gold was a bit of a contradiction
in terms, but also a compliment: Buried with the deceased,
it indicated that the departed had been a man or woman
of "shining or golden spirit"—sort of an American Express Gold
Card to ensure spiritual credit in the land beyond the grave.

Sail-planes were invented again and again as toys throughout
the world. But because they did not contain propulsive motors—
gliders in your culture were developed only *after* the perfection
of motor-propelled aircraft—such devices were always relegated
to children. Being of light fabric and structure, they seldom
survived very long,when buried with the dead—except when rep-
licated in metal, as in the examples that prompted your question.

*The Piri Ri'es Map, found in a library in Turkey, depicts the
coastline of Antarctica, now completely covered by ice. Some
experts believe the land seems to have been surveyed from the air.
When was the original map drawn?*

When Antarctica was ice-free and the North Pole was located
in the present Sahara. Your scientists can best tell you exactly
when that was: Inhabitants of the time did not calculate that
they were living so many thousands of years before Christ.

Even had the ancient peoples possessed flying craft, they
would have not needed them to draft such maps as you describe, since they shared a rather tedious but ingenious form
of surveying that enabled them to map *as if* from the air.

Briefly, it worked as follows: Observers would be placed on
significant, mutually visible landmarks—say, on the crown of a
high hill and on the cusp of a bare, sandy peninsula—and told
to wait for a given astronomical event: the occlusion of a star
or the achievement of sunrise or sunset. At that instant, measure-
ments would graph the direction of shadows cast by the sun
or moon at the exact spot where the observer was standing.

By lighting simultaneous signal fires that could be seen from
one observation point to another—and by having observers mark

the shadows cast by *those* lights—rather accurate angles could be determined between any given landmark and the sun or moon. Simple geometric fiddling, such as any 8-year-old could accomplish, quickly established the exact angles and distances between landmarks. Repeated observations corrected one another, and eventually, very accurate maps could be assembled.

Even then it was known that rays of the sun and moon are practically parallel—which was positive proof of these bodies' divinity. After all, a mortal's cooking fire casts rays that diverge from their source. The sun was *seen* to have diverging rays when setting, yet its rays could be proven to be parallel—a paradox explicable only by the divine whim of a sustained miracle. And you wonder why the sun was universally seen as a supernatural being, and why the world became more "secular" upon the discovery of one-point perspective?

These surveying techniques antedate the coming of the last Ice Age across Europe. They were developed not long after the domestication of fire, were handed down and traded among peoples, and were used in Africa well over 100,000 years ago.

Did Atlantean technology overstep itself, just as our 20th-century science seems likely to do? What part does the myth of Atlantis play in our present group destiny?

The Atlantean civilization lasted many centuries, yet your imaginations focus only on its last gasp, evading the insight that science *cannot* overstep itself—not without a human pushing it from behind, as when your movie-mythologies depict scientists raising monsters from the depths of the sea. To be cruel or foolish, you do not need a laser beam. You can be just as rash with a boomerang as with an atom bomb. Do not blame your President or your Pentagon for what you wish to eradicate from yourselves. When you—as individuals and as a civilization—can honestly say, "We wish no one harm," the world in which war is necessary, or defenses against it desirable, will fall away from you.

You will distance yourself from the world of war by never overstepping your *thoughts*. I can never repeat too often that evil equals inability, for that equation is more important for your civilization than $E=mc^2$!

*Over the past few years, a number of alternative healing energies
have been introduced. Are these really new, or manifestations
of ancient practices?*

As a race, you are learning to appreciate a wider spectrum
of wisdoms and disciplines. Analogy time: For many centuries,
Egyptian hieroglyphics were a closed book. Not until the
Rosetta Stone came to light were your scientists and lin-
guists able to decipher the cartouches lining the obelisks and
tombs of Egypt, which can now be read with alacrity.

What changed? The sensitivity of individuals to that which
was there all along. The healing energies you speak of have been
here all along, and now—fortunately—you are beginning to
widen your definition of *healing.* A century ago, a healing
substance was something from the druggist that tasted bad and
made your body react violently. You now understand that fresh
water, and a good diet are health-promoting. Approval, affection,
and acts of kindness are old hat, but your appreciation of their virtue has increased. More and more is found to be therapeutic!

The more you widen your possibilities of what may be—
in healing, or endeavors of any sort—the more you will find to
back up your case. Do not assume that everything has been
figured out in the remote past, nor that the secrets you so badly
need must *wait* to be discovered. You need assume only that
energies already here can be newly interpreted by you, *as
individuals*, to answer the questions you have been posing for
so long. Look in different places, therefore, for your answers.

*Can you give us a reason for the current epidemic of Unicorn-
omania? Did such a single-horned beastie ever really exist?*

As a flesh-and-blood creature, no. As a quite-living emblem
of certain aspirations and ambitions of your race, most certainly.

It will not surprise you that the unicorn's horn proceeds
in a twirl outward from the region of the forehead contain-
ing the third eye. The unicorn is basically a whitewashed,
sanitized, spiritualized version of the horse, which animal
has a long and beloved association with mankind.

Originally, the unicorn was a symbol for the higher powers
and "finer" nature accessible to Man once he had purged from

his body consciousness the "lower" animal impulses of sex, gluttony, and territoriality. Many of the unicorn's alleged traits —being rare, elusive, solitary, and a denizen of exotic lands— bear out this interpretation. But like so many other trans- cendental symbols—like the Philosopher's Stone that turns all substances to gold, like the physical resurrection of the body on some as-yet-unnamed day—the unicorn deftly escaped its ivory tower to run wild in the popular imagination.

If the animal has been sighted time and again, this is not the first time that you have used the cookie-cutter of a given symbol to carve your external reality into bite-size morsels.

What was the purpose of human sacrifice in the Aztec culture?

Your anthropologists can answer this more fully than I can. Simply, the Aztecs believed that the sun had to be appeased with human hearts, or it would sulk beneath the horizon and not rise again to create the day.

Beneath such an "explanation," however, lurks an even more barbaric misconception that persists into your present day: the belief that certain forces are out to get you, and you must appease them by some kind of sacrifice. The hefty insurance premiums many of your cities pay out are just such a sacrifice, intended to keep lawsuits at bay. In a strange and amusing way, the very abundance of insurance money has brought about increasingly generous jury awards in damage-claim cases.

Similarly, the increase in number of victims sacrificed to the Sun God did not allay the anxiety in the hearts of the Aztecs. They saw that the Sun simply took these extra portions —these second helpings—as Its divine due, not bothering to shine any brighter or rise any earlier. That the Sun God made no gesture of thanks or even of acknowledgment made the human sacrifices seem inadequate somehow—and only increased the priests' despair: If the Sun were that much of a glutton, how could It ever be appeased, ever satiated?

In short, images of greed you have conjured up will auto- matically seek to consume more and more. If you believe that your needs for power and electricity must increase, then so they shall—without your discovering any other sources of natural, efficient, non-polluting power that might supplant them.

What do discarnates think of the cruelty that Man has inflicted since he first became a thinking being and thus, top dog in the animal kingdom?

We view cruelty for what it basically is—a clumsy attempt to create instant power by causing the suffering, and hence abasement, of another life form. Cruelty is practiced precisely because the inflicter does *not* consider himself to be "top dog," and usually has quite good reasons for that poor opinion!

Those who are cruel are not necessarily uncivilized or even unenlightened. But they suffer from a bad self-image that, when regarded with the inward eyes of the self, is found wanting. On a scale of 1 to 10, they measure themselves as a 4. To increase their relative self-worth, they choose another human being or animal who cannot fight back and reduce it to a 2 or a 1 on that same scale. By inflicting suffering, the inflicters see themselves as more fortunate—and thus, superior—by comparison.

It is like throwing mud upon your neighbor's garment, rather than taking time to launder your own. But that frivolous simile in no way begins to communicate the degree and depth of cruelty that has been practiced down through your centuries. Again, the practitioner of cruelty does not, at bottom, like himself. He inflicts on others, outwardly, the same torments he has suffered inwardly, in silence. Cruelty, in a way, is a nasty form of self-deception: "Because I do not feel *his* pain, it is doing *me* no harm."

With some sorrow, I must point out that the person who asked this question* has, more than once, inflicted deliberate cruelties on members of his own family, enjoying making others squirm as a way of showing others who is boss. And so, he has raised the question of cruelty for much the same reason that others project their inward sufferings outward upon unwilling victims. By asking the question, he wishes to exteriorize his inward pain.

Thus, there is another serious aspect to cruelty that I must discuss. It would be bad enough if the atrocity ended with the victim's death, with the torturer repenting and matured, never again to enter erroneous ways. But unfortunately, certain minds tend to *dwell* on cruelty, hoarding up the past's brutal excesses as

---

Howard M. Mossman, the channel's late father.

an excuse to distrust humanity. Your Mark Twain adopted this pose with a sense of irony, but others do so in utter seriousness—and willingly distract themselves from the abundant compassion, love, warmth, and kindnesses that are even more multitudinous in the history of mankind.

Cruelties are typically—*intentionally*—theatrical. They would lose much of their impact if they did not conspicuously, consciously violate an accepted standard of conduct. But their garish spectacle makes them seem more numerous than they are in reality. For every bullfight, a hundred kittens have been petted and played with. For every execution, a thousand babies have been cooed over and hugged with loving pride. And to so imbalance the accounts of the universe by perverse insistence on its lesser aspects is a serious form of cruelty-to-self.

Ironically, some secretly need cruel people to compare themselves with, for much the same reasons that those cruel people inflicted their indignities in the first place. You need not inflict cruelties in order to feel superior. You need only point to a Nazi—or to the Plains Indians, Pontius Pilate, or a gang of little boys—and declare that *you* would never stoop to such barbarities! But dwelling on past injustice demands that sins must return on the inflicters' heads so that *they* feel the sharp sword of suffering and deprivation. Thus, a pessimistic, bitter reflecting on Man's lesser nature perpetuates exactly the kind of atrocity that the brooders claim to condemn!

Cruelty does have its own built-in punishment, of course: By inflicting it, you imply that you are *not* part of the universe on which you inflict pain. In effect, you amputate a portion of your greater being every time you inflict hurt upon another. And thus, on a spiritual level, the worst monsters of your history have literally rendered themselves deaf, dumb, blind, and limbless. Mental cruelty can be just as devastating, which explains why those who sneer and belittle frequently find themselves "cut off" from those with whom they would prefer to maintain contact.

I have said what evil truly is—inability. Nowhere is the equation more obvious than in the infliction of cruelty: He who cannot win his fellow man's agreement by logic and diplomacy can always burn him at the stake. But that immolation is always a second option, after a better and more benign attempt at interaction has failed miserably!

The Bible mentions Mary Magdalene only in passing. Can you tell us more about her?

I must preface my answer with one of my famous analogies! In your filmed biographies of individuals who actually lived, a number of characters are often combined into one for the sake of dramatic expediency. It is also normal for a screenwriter to combine real-life incidents and create imaginary dialogue that *might* have been spoken. It is even possible, as in the case of George Washington and the cherry tree, for myths about real-life personages to spring up shortly after their lifetime.

With that understanding, you will not be surprised that Mary Magdalene in your New Testament is a composite of a number of women known to have consorted with Christ, and who have been combined into one woman to make the "story" easier to handle—both theologically and in dramatic terms.

You would easily accept that Christ did not heal *only* those individuals cited in the Bible. He did tend to consort with what were, in those days, considered the lower classes. Women at the time were rather restricted if they chose to be respectable, but whores and keepers of inns and brothels enjoyed a certain freedom—and admiration, because they had psychological understanding that many of their respectable sisters utterly lacked. They were feared and envied, then, by women who played by the rules. For that reason, Gospel writers knew that their story would "play" better with only a single prostitute in the cast.

Is the increase in Satanism leading to a time when Satan will ultimately rule the world?

In the first place, there is no increase in Satanism, nor is Satanism a movement *per se.* Your newspaper journalists do an increasingly efficient job of reporting on rituals that smack of Satanism, and your popular fictions give the impression that Satanism—or black witchcraft, if you prefer—is an efficient means of obtaining what one wants.

The problem is age-old: People see themselves as powerless, so they assign to a supernatural being—God, Satan, a saint or deva—power that they should rightly seek within themselves. Projecting this power outward *does* sometimes free it of emotional constraints, so participants in these rituals often can claim results. But so can anyone who trusts in his or her ability to create a chosen reality without outside intervention.

I find appeals to Satan rather amusing: The petitioners believe that Satan, in the Number 2 seat, is more motivated than God—and inclined to try harder. They intuit that they do not deserve that which they ask for, and so think they stand a better chance of obtaining it on the "black market," so to speak. That they enter upon such transactions with these beliefs helps explain why black witchcraft often has unpleasant side effects—which are accepted as part of the bargain, much as patients accept a bitter pill on the assumption that a pleasant remedy would have no effect.

Your historians have pointed out that Satanism is merely an inversion of Christianity—a ritual based on another ritual, and not directly related to any external reality of the unseen world. Were Satanism *really* a repudiation of Christianity, it might have struck out on its own and made its mark on the world. But because it shares in the belief of sacrifice, that one must suffer or give up something to achieve anything, it is wholly bound to its original parent. Thus, it attracts those of the same temperament as those who manipulate unseen entities by praying religiously in church.

None of your world religions evolved during a period of democracy. All of them, therefore, preserve to a greater or lesser degree the distortions of hierarchal, hereditary government. Only in recent years has God been thought to have "chosen" or "appointed" Jesus as the Christ; before, his lineage—both from the Royal House of David and from the Holy Ghost—gave him legitimate title to the Throne of Heaven.

And not just Christianity is afflicted with this distortion. Hinduism, Buddhism, and any number of other sects have "Lords" who in effect "own" their worshippers, even as medieval Tsars did their serfs. The theological opinion that God must look down His nose at humanity is a direct result of this projection of royalty upon All That Is: Since kings took great pains to maintain their distance from the rabble, God must be an even greater snob! Only with this separation of the divine from the human does the concept of original sin remotely begin to make sense.

You cannot trust a tyrant to have your best interests at heart. Thus, your approach to such a being must be one of fulsome praise and supplication. If any healthy human were treated to such groveling and flattery, he or she would soon tire of it—yet you expect God to sit there and simply lap it up for eternity!

Only an insecure satrap would have his head turned by constant hymns of praise. Any truly superior being would much rather enter into a state of *friendship* with Man, even as you do with pet dogs and cats and, to a more relevant extent, with your children. You love pets and children for what they are, not because they lick your hand or purchase lavish Mother's or Father's Day cards. Yet there is no question who is superior in the relationship: Much of the love you receive is based on an acknowledgment of your greater wisdom and ability.

You may believe that Satan, being understandably insecure, would fall for such ego-boosting folderol. But Satan is more or less an allegory or personification of certain human traits and tendencies that are usually worked through in adolescence, at the very latest. To a large degree, devil-worshippers try to recapture—or in many cases, experience for the first time— the leaving-of-the-nest rebellion intended to thrust adolescents out into the world to seek their own challenges.

You can easily become obsessed with various fulcrums of emotional development, and thus much of your fearful admiration for the teenage rebel enters into your Satanic mythology.

Yes, Satan is "real," in the same sense that Santa Claus or the Easter Bunny has an enduring place in the popular psyche. But just as a man in a red suit on a street corner at Christmas is no proof of Santa Claus's existence, neither are some rather hair-raising episodes in the history of the Church evidence for more than a masquerade by discarnate entities. You enjoy dressing up and adopting the trappings of figures from popular culture, and discarnates share in similar pleasures. But because our choices of costume are often quite imaginative, you may find yourself in the dilemma of a small child at Christmastime, unable to distinguish adult play-acting from adult-inspired fantasy.

Did Francis Bacon write the plays of Shakespeare?

The argument that Shakespeare did not write the plays bearing his name arises from the assumption that a country boy from Stratford could not have known all that is shown in his plays—tales of statecraft and insights into how sophisticated monarchs behave. Class structure is rather endemic in England, such that some find it difficult to assume that anyone not of the peerage could have written anything worth reading.

Shakespeare's secret, if one can call it that, was being able to look past prejudice and class structure and observe what is human—and thereby, dramatic and enthralling—in all men, whether peasants or monarchs, kings or kitchen maids. His affection for, if not always approval of, his characters cuts through all his work like a bright cord of feeling and aliveness.

Because Shakespeare did not make the mistake that many of his later critics made, he is the one you read today. If Francis Bacon wrote Shakespeare, why aren't you reading Francis Bacon?

Was Shakespeare a channel?

In terms of your question, no—the plays did not come through him automatically. I want to explain the process he *did* use, for many of you can use it for your own endeavors.

The process is simply this: Say, "All human experience is accessible to me. Just what I need for my creative endeavors will automatically be given." Of course, that is a positive paraphrase of the old Latin line, "Nothing human is alien to me."

On his own, Shakespeare witnessed some strange occurrences —so very strange that he knew they would not play in Peoria, let alone in the Globe Theatre. And so he resorted—or reverted— to the conventions of received wisdom and popular knowledge. But those of you who have seen *Hamlet* will understand that the ghost of Hamlet's father is being channeled by Hamlet when it communicates; and is otherwise operating as an apparition. Do not suppose that the next production of *Hamlet* will be using a Ouija board instead of Yorick's skull—but read the ghost scene as a channeled experience, and it makes infinitely better sense!

You will find more than so-called occult knowledge in Shakespeare, for he had a great advantage that many of you do not: His theatrical profession allowed him to push the truth to whatever extreme was most effective. He was not out to write good plays, but to entertain an audience who had the afternoon off and desperately needed escape, thrills, exaltation, and a thumping good ending. He did that as well as he knew how, which was pretty damn well.

His point of view—his way of entering his creative state—was what made him so successful, though he is not the only individual who has used it. Many of you can—and have!

Historians are always disagreeing, even about the fairly recent past. Would you mind refereeing some of their disputes?

I'm afraid so, because to do so would be counter-productive to the growth of your species as a whole.

Over time, your vision of the past will change because *you* have changed. If one single and immutable truth is to be held down through the ages, for you to worship or deplore, then to that degree, you are imaginatively constrained, unable to sift the past for significant fragments that might be of far greater use in the current challenges you face.

As just one example, the question of what killed off the dinosaurs has been "answered" by the hypothesis of sudden climactic change—a scenario that imaginatively prefigured the greenhouse effect that your scientists are rightly beginning to fear. Again and again, you seize on those shards of the past's shattered mirror that glint and reflect back to your present position, conveniently and *necessarily* ignoring what does not sparkle enough to catch your fancy.

Myth, you might say, is sometimes too vast to emulate—you find it vain to attempt to surpass a Shakespeare or an Alexander. But lesser figures of history serve, you might say, as compost heaps and trellises for growth of your present ambitions and understanding. And unless large tracts of the past are left fallow and empty, your imaginations are not going to be able to range and graze fully. For example, if the secrets of the Pyramids were common knowledge, then your archaeologists and engineers and mystics would lose a potent challenge. If the motivations and psychology of Cleopatra or Henry VIII were known to the last jot, what a tragedy for your novelists and screenwriters!

Rest assured that any historical error will automatically correct itself in the light of new understandings. But even historical misconceptions can, however briefly, impel you to create new and praiseworthy *current* history of your own.

Why does Man seem doomed to learn through trial and error?
Can't some teacher give us a lesson that will finally "take"?

No lesson can be truly assimilated unless it is *felt* on all levels—intellectually, emotionally, and spiritually. And unless you experience both the positive and negative sides of a given "fact," then part of the larger picture is missing.

In your world, those who are naively optimistic without cause are often treated with contempt, as not worth listening to. That is your innate instinct at play. Not that one needs suffer to become wise, but to learn, one must have reacted to *both* attractive and disagreeable stimuli *as well as to the same stimuli in both positive and negative ways.*

Do you see a parallel with that statement and the procedures of your so-called scientific method? Very good, then you are catching on!

When I say that Man's earlier mistakes are "divine," I mean that they have been the means by which he attains divinity. Christianity enshrined the concept of the fortunate fall—that without Adam's sin, Christ would have been unable to redeem mankind. I am here to tell you that *there is nothing wrong with making a mistake*, as long as you do not let the mistake become so tangled in your ego that it winds up on—or as a hole in—your résumé.

View your past errors—personally, and as a species—as "experiments" that yielded data you could have arrived at by no other means. Then the idea of waste, loss, and tragedy takes on far less force. Just as a great artist may be fascinated by a physically imperfect model and thus get a clearer concept of "regular" anatomy, so would it be impossible for you to get a true view of your world from only a straight and narrow path.

I am not giving you *carte blanche* to do what you know or believe to be wrong. I am promising—not warning, *promising*—that as you evolve, your concept of what is no longer desirable or permissible will expand rather drastically. If you hold onto your antiquated concepts of guilt and atonement, then you are going to have one hell of a karmic debt when your bills come due at the end of the Cosmic Month!

Realizing that you were wrong is half the battle. Victory comes when you see not only *why* you were wrong, but *how to live so that the previous error is wholly detoured* and a new, more workable approach to life is followed. Apologizing for spilling your drink will not blot up the stain. The not-so-hidden "assignment" of such a *faux pas* is not just learning to clean up after yourself, but how to more deftly maneuver your drink in the first place.

Look at your past errors and ignorances as blanks in a larger fresco of knowledge—areas absent of concept and color that simply begged to be filled in. The empty spaces in a stamp album send you out with renewed ambition to obtain (and experience!) the missing rarities, not to ask forgiveness that there are so many stamps missing in the early pages of your "historical" Album of Mankind.

A parting note: In both your Eastern and Western mythologies, many gods are guilty of extraordinary lapses of judgment, morality, and compassion. Their shortcomings were not intended to make them loom any less godlike in their worshippers' eyes, but rather were imagined—and related—in the hopes that such a spectacular boo-boo, committed by a divine being, would warn off mortals tempted to run a similar experiment.

The "innocent" mistakes committed in your various fairy tales are other examples of the strength and usefulness of mythic error, which also explains the innate psychological popularity of the Easter legend—merely a variation on the old theme of "When a god is punished, it reminds us little godlings to mind our p's and q's."

3

Your Thought-Created World

*• The Bermuda Triangle explained by consensus reality
• Where personal reality ends • Coordinate points and
how to use them • The meaning of coincidence • Basic
mechanics of apports • Wealth and abundance as your
natural birthrights—and how to claim them*

*What happens to the planes and ships that vanish in the
Bermuda Triangle?*

I do not have any personal knowledge of this. There are black
holes, you might say, in my knowledge. I will withdraw for
a time, seek out information, come back with it later—if that
would be acceptable . . .

As far as your Bermuda Triangle is concerned: If you look
at a map of the undersea bottom, you'll see nothing particularly
untoward there. Nor are magnetic storms the root of the problem;
if they were, your instruments would have detected them.

What, then, will explain these disappearances? Consensual
reality! You in this room agree on many details: the color of the
carpet, the temperature of the air, the quality of my voice.
Let's say you were out in the desert, however, without others
with whom you could compare notes. Removed from the bol-
ster of your fellow humans' experience, you could get in
touch with realities that are by no means "common" in the dull
sense of that word. Not only are they *un*common realities, but
they are hardly shared by a majority of your nation—or your
species.

For initiation and spiritual growth, North American Indians
would go out alone into the wilderness where the consensual
reality of the tribe could not exercise so strong an effect. And
in that wilderness, in those lonely hours, our young brave—or
in biblical times, our lone prophet—would experience energies
and realities quite different from that experienced by his

nation as a whole. But he could return, of course, to revitalize his group with his new, uncommon impressions.

A former client of ours had a father in the military, stationed in Utah, where planes regularly disappeared over a certain area of desert. No trace whatsoever! Many top-secret devices were brought in, but it was a bit of an embarrassment for the government—to our friend's knowledge, nothing was ever found.

Long before your civilization was, much of the area of the Bermuda Triangle was dry ground and largely waste—a desert where shamans of the time went for initiation. If you look upon your maps now, it is again a wasteland, but now of water.

When out of sight of land, you are out of touch with your fellow men's consensual realities. Specifically, in your Bermuda Triangle and in areas of the American desert, there are the equivalent of—I have to choose my words carefully from our friend's vocabulary—what I would call *accelerations of time.*

Normally, time is "level," and yet there are areas where it accelerates exponentially. If you hit the right spot at the right "time," it is as if there were a black hole in space—and there are black holes in time as well. A plane going into the Bermuda Triangle under such conditions would not notice anything amiss, for such time anomalies—which also produce shamanistic phenomenon in certain holy spots—do not show up on your instruments.

From the pilots' point of view, they flew their mission successfully and returned to base. However, the day on which they returned—this is difficult to explain—lay in their *present*; and yet they had literally accelerated into your future. They came back to a future that does not exist now. In other words, they returned to a probable base.

Such wholesale disappearances into Probabilityville are not that infrequent. Many of so-called missing children have turned a corner, gone to their probable school, and come home to eat a probable supper—in a slightly different reality. Several individuals in this room have "disappeared" from what they thought was their past. They are still being mourned Back When, but consider themselves quite alive— in *this* probable corner of the universe.

Because this may make you somewhat paranoid, I wish to assure you that intent is always operative. Pilots who are "lost" quite often need an acceleration, you might say, in their lives. Not that their planes were lost in the Bermuda Triangle, so much as *they* lost the world they left. Their intent was to escape from the rigors of the military Notice the paradox and the parallel: Children who are over-disciplined, soldiers whose basic intents are stifled, disappear thus. Their longing for a different consensual reality automatically gives them the "ability" to seek out such anomalies.

If you want an acceleration, an automobile accident can flip you, momentarily, into a more advantageous "spot." Again, this kind of psychological *and literal* time-acceleration is by no means uncommon. Almost everyone knows a friend or relative who's aged literally overnight. In a very short time, this individual has become older—has taken a quantum leap down the path of physical life.

This happens regularly, but your consensual beliefs about reality force you to overlook such changes—which, however, are registered quite clearly and dramatically on your subconscious. This is why individuals so often feel emotions quite inappropriate to the life going on around them: They are reacting to realities that the social consensus tends to blot out. But if you are quite happy with your lives, growing and fulfilling yourselves, you are not likely to walk into a time warp. And so, you may rest easy.

If I go out in a field and throw a baseball, that's my *reality. But if others come onto the field with me, they can create a reality of their own. They can throw my ball back or let it drop—and can end their interactions with me at any point. Where does my free will end and others' begin?*

Your throwing-the-ball analogy is excellent, and I can now begin to weave a comprehensible pattern, using your loom.

Imagine that everyone on the field has decided to play baseball. Therefore, certain "choices" are automatically not going to manifest themselves. If you bat that ball, for instance, you will find everyone in the outfield is motivated to catch it in their gloves. Certain general desires—intents, now—have been agreed upon, consciously or otherwise.

A discussion group, for instance, is all pulling in the same direction. When your group gets together, there is a feeling of happy discovery and inquiry in the air. You share your energy in a *controlled* exhilaration and do not find yourselves in chaos, even when things get raucous and lively. You have decided upon a similar game, scoring points—individually and as a team—for everyone's benefit.

Yes, free will does apply, but free will is not chaotic! On the baseball diamond, you do not have one person show up in a football helmet, another one on hockey skates and a third with water wings. Because you—individually, in groups, and as a race—decide in advance what game you are going to play, things stay on a more even keel than they otherwise might.

This is where many of your philosophers fall onto the horns of their dilemma. It may *appear* that free will is circumscribed in such cases. Yet, as you well know, there are an infinite number of daubs a brush can make upon a canvas. Any game can be played an infinite number of ways. There only *seems* to be a paradox of "Is there free will or is there not?"

A great deal depends, as I said, on agreement. When there are two sets of rules, almost inevitably the game becomes a lot less fun. Now, a questing nature is the basic "rule" that almost all of you started out with in this life. If you did not start with it, you adopted it since! That rule brings you together with other "players" from various parts of the country. They have warmed up under different circumstances but, after scoring the same goals, can appreciate your individual performance as no one else could.

If you see that you are automatically surrounded by teammates—or by opposing players who, even though they outlaw your kick, are still playing by rules you all agree upon—then you will see through the apparent paradox.

How can we become more aware of coordinate points and utilize their energy?

Perhaps the first question would be, "What *is* a coordinate point to begin with?"

Imagine a three-dimensional grid. Those of you who took geometry will have no trouble with this; those who as joyful children climbed on jungle gyms will have no problem. Where a vertical rod intersects two horizontal rods at right angles, you have a nexus of several dimensions. Imagine other intersections—of radial waves of energy of different frequencies—passing through the same juncture, and you have a rough approximation of a coordinate point.

You know coordinate points by other names: chakras, vortexes of energy, centers of gravity, ley lines. Physical reality takes advantage of them in order to express itself—but coordinate points are not eternal, as you may have thought.

A coordinate point is not only where a number of energies come together, but a nexus of opportunities where you may enter from one angle and leave on another. Coordinate points are sources of energy, "banks" where you can make withdrawals from a literally inexhaustible account. They are also foreign-exchange bureaus where you can—to use an analogy—convert your lire into Deutschmarks or into a "common currency" of energy, spontaneity, and enjoyment which, I promise you, is accepted in all corners of your universe.

How, then, do you take advantage of this multifaceted bundle—quiver, shall we say?—of opportunities, which itself quivers with life? Examine your own intent! Is there anything you wish to change? Do you simply wish to expand and become more of what you truly are? You may want to feel more mountain air in your lungs; or to feel the joyous blood coursing through the smallest of your capillaries; or feel the love that is eternally a part of your being but which, because of your incarnate neurological structure, you experience only intermittently.

To digress for a moment: You are surrounded by air, and yet you cannot inhale non-stop. So you experience air only briefly and intermittently, when you breathe in. Now, many can teach you how to breathe more effectively; and others will teach you how to accept and experience that love which, you might say, comprises the entire jungle gym. But the teachers most important to you are the others crawling on the jungle gym, for as you watch their spectacular monkeyshines, you discover your own latent capabilities, as well as where you might like to wind up.

To find a coordinate point, first find out where you are now: Are you ambitious, anxious, sad, impatient? Analyze your condition spiritually—or however you wish to measure yourself, for you have as many parameters and axes as the universe itself. You are a universe in miniature. So, which angle of attack do you wish to take?

Ideally, go out of doors. Just as you need not visit a power station to run your hair dryer, so you need not look for a big coordinate point. If do you need a 4,000-mile pilgrimage to a major coordinate point, you will be led there automatically. Meanwhile, if you need only a small outlet to brew your morning coffee, there are plenty to be found. Your own intuition, coupled with your intent, will lead you to the nearest local source.

It does not hurt to go where there are constant winds, especially where rocks come together to form a pinnacle. Such places, if not coordinate points, often fall on the axes that some of you know as ley lines. There, you can plug in your personal energy and run whatever "appliance" suits your fancy. But the refreshing energy to which *you* are led may not be the same that your brother or sister can make use of.

I've come across areas in Los Angeles where I felt spinning or whirling sensations. Were those coordinate points, or was I given the wrong information?

All information given out in this world is right! The question is, *to whom* or *for whom* is it correct? All information has upon it an address and a Zip Code, you might say, and sometimes also a Social Security number. So if I give you information that does not seem to have your name on it—if it does not open the petals of your soul gratefully; if my truth does not make you long for another helping—by all means keep searching.

Whirling sensations are the result of your own *reaction to* or perception of a coordinate point. As you know, whirling frequently betokens change, rotation, revolution—in the political sense as well. If you come upon an opportunity for change, but you see change as threatening, you may indeed find yourself light-headed, as if poised over a great abyss where a sudden movement could fling you down into its maw.

Change can take place in the absence of a coordinate point, just as a hive of bees need not be situated in a bed of flowers.

I have noticed a flurry of coincidences lately. Is there any meaning to them?

Yes. As when your TV set crackles when an appliance is plugged in or when you see lightning flashing among the clouds, connections are being made so that energy can flow. Basically, coincidences are signs of a coming change in your personal weather.

The changes so indicated, I might add, are always healthy, the transformations always beneficial. Even if no outward change comes from this flow of energy, at least your daily life will take on a grace, ease, and spontaneity it did not have before. So look for coincidences to be the forerunners of pleasant changes or of deepening abilities on your part.

Before my wife left for Florida, she asked, "Have you seen my enamelware skillet?" I looked under the bed, in the closets, even in the refrigerator, but it was not in the apartment.

When she got back, she asked, "Where did you find my skillet? I looked in the cabinet, and there it was!"

But I searched that cabinet after she left! It wasn't there, and I didn't put it there. I figure it must have fallen into a time warp—and hope you can explain what happened to it.

Your question presupposes that such unusual occurrences are exceptions or overrides to the normal rules of physics. You are used to seeing objects disappear when you heave them into the garbage or burn them in the fireplace, but when an object vanishes or re-creates itself *abruptly*, you prick up your ears.

Even as certain chemical reactions can be accelerated by powerful sources of energy, so can the time necessary for an object to change its state be reduced to next to nothing. But sources of empowering energy are not *necessarily* to be found in your physical reality.

Imagine yourself as a fish in a clear mountain stream. Time, as you recognize it, flows always in one direction—

downhill—and it is hard for you to imagine a world in which
the prevailing current flows in a contrary direction. Because
of the contours of the riverbank and bottom, however, there
will be pools where the current may wash back upon itself, to
a point where there may seem to be no current at all. Thus, in
your own world, you have places where time does not
sweep things away quite so quickly—languid whirlpools of
the spirit, where physical objects will persist in fresh condition for century upon century, without change.

Your medievalists bemoan that modern air pollution has
destroyed carvings that endured the storms and summers of the
open air since before your Renaissance. But I tell you, rather,
the acceleration of the modern industrial age, the searching
for faster methodologies and decisive change, have altered
the "current" of your collective time. Many stagnant time-
pools, which used to eddy harmlessly around cathedrals and
other revered monuments of the past, were "straightened
out" and swept away; and with them went the preservative
effect upon the particular monuments they enclosed. No
coincidence, then, that destruction of art and architecture has
historically coincided with a "breath of fresh air" in terms of
thought, philosophy, and world-view—your First World War
being a prime example of one such change of current.

Now, back to our streambed analogy: Whether you choose
to swim upstream or down, the rate at which you move is
entirely controlled by the speed of the current. If it is flowing
too quickly, you may—like a spawning salmon—have to jump
out of "time" entirely in order to make any progress. To a
degree, you are all swimming upstream to "spawn," to
multiply yourselves in the original clear spring in which
you first found your being. But in general—*in general*, now
—as long as you are within time, its speed assures that you
will perhaps be able to hold your place, as in dreams or in
meditative states, but not travel backwards against the
current except by a heroic flip of your tail!

A fish readily accepts submerged rocks and logs as part of
its natural world. Above, where the water's surface interfaces
with the air, is a shimmering and seemingly illusory curtain.
Things on the other side are demonstrably "real," yet appear
distorted. They are not what they seem to be, for when one

of them enters the water-reality, it abruptly changes its appearance. If you were a fish, you would be amazed by the sight of a dragonfly who could "swim" not only upstream but—get this!—*across* the stream without having to tack for correction. Now, say that the dragonfly is laying eggs, dropping them in short bounces as its abdomen contacts the water's surface. You can understand the amazement of the trout who watches such a miracle in progress: Tiny eggs, entering the water from a different reality!

The circumference of the trout's world is determined by the amount of water in the stream. In a season of drought when the water is low, certain objects—an overhanging branch, say—may be withdrawn entirely from the watery reality. In periods of flood, water creeps up the stream's banks, including previously dry land in the trout's reality. Objects captured by high waters upstream are floated down, and the trout confronts all kinds of strange objects that make no sense in an underwater context. In a very real sense, your UFO flaps occur during periods of "floodtide." You might say that UFOs are objects that float through your reality, having no real purpose, much less origin, there.

In times of "low water," you will feel yourself emotionally and spiritually drained—pun intended! While the physical streambed of your life may not have changed, your freedom within it is restricted, just as our trout's freedom is diminished when the level of the river is reduced. In such constricted circumstances, things take on a closer, harsher, more immediate tone. You feel cramped and thirstily await the breaking of the dam that will return your potential to its full surge.

If you think that your emotions are intimately linked with the flow of time in your immediate vicinity, you are absolutely right. Why else, during periods of happiness, does the very fabric of life seem more spacious and your options more varied? And why does mental pain or discomfort slow time so drastically?

Now, to return to our subject: apported objects! If you give enough of a push to a pencil or saucepan, you could indeed flip it out of the "water" which you inhabit. It might skip along the surface—upstream, now—and drift back into your reality a few moments "later." Or, if it skipped downstream, it might re-emerge into the water so distantly that you could not perceive it. It might even land on the riverbank, not to reappear until times of flood lifted it free again.

You must realize that the "energy" or "push" given such an object is, of course, essentially emotional. An object that appears and disappears is not *necessarily* something you strongly like or dislike. Rather, an *emotionally vacant* object is more likely to be the butt of such poltergeistish pranks. Otters and water polo players do not attach much importance to the inflatable balls they buffet about. Similarly, you usually choose to vent your emotional excesses on some object that, for you, *contains less emotion than it normally should.* It cannot break your heart if it is damaged in the process. Thus, it is more buoyant and easier to manipulate.

Shouldn't those same emotional principles apply to people and friendships as well as objects?

Of course! All objects and entities are, to a degree, condensations of a larger field. Walk through a meadow when dawn is breaking, and you will see spiderwebs and leaves of grass bejeweled with dewdrops—which have condensed out of the general "field" of water vapor in the air.

Now, just as a snowflake may grow in the air or evaporate back into its original vapor, depending on the relative humidity and density of moisture in the surrounding cloud, so do the "clouds" of your events—and daily lives—swell, move, and dissipate according to the matrix of generally invisible "vapor" and the influx of energy in which they find themselves immersed. Dropping a snowflake on a red-hot stove will vaporize it in an instant, whereas filling a metal pot with liquid nitrogen would swiftly cause the metal to grow frosty whiskers from water vapor previously present but—unless the air be extremely humid—virtually imperceptible to your physical senses.

I do not wish to frighten you, but each and every one of you is quite literally surrounded by any number of fields —"vapors" of different kinds, you might say—which may or may not manifest or "condense." Physical love is one such field. As more attention and energy are poured into that probable event, the opportunity of meeting another individual is the first to "condense." If you meet someone after twenty years and not before, *it is literally true that this person had not "condensed"—and thus did not exist—up until that moment,* as far as you are concerned. And vice versa: Each of you inhabited separate, if parallel, universes whose characteristics were similar enough for you to believe they were one and the same. But quite literally, you two did not exist for one another until your mutual interface "condensed."

You can see why relationships live and die according to the amount of emotional energy one devotes to them. Of course, either partner may "pull the plug" and break the connection, so that the manifested relationship automatically dissolves back into its original field—whereupon other people, perhaps more eager for intimacy, will add to their own emotional constructions the field's increased supply of "vapor." And so, like icicles that hang from your eaves every winter, certain relationships and events may display seasonal or periodic regularity, "evaporating" during unfavorable circumstances and re-forming themselves when conditions are appropriate—perhaps a few years hence, perhaps in an adjacent life.

So not only your physical objects "get lost"—so do events! The horrors and fears of your childhood have, I trust, been washed ashore, beached where they can no longer bother you.

To return to apports: Many things you cannot find again after a move and but do not truly miss are victims of this kind of emotional forgetfulness. After your attention-energy withdraws from them, they literally dissipate, having been vulnerable and impermanent to begin with.

Not that you must keep a watchful vigil over your homes, lest the floors fade away and the walls begin to un-wall themselves. Nor must you hold the contents of your closet in perfect imaginative focus, lest your wardrobe drift away during the night! Rather, I am saying that the object that is emotionally neutral—or which holds *less emotion* than its "capacity" would indicate—is the candidate most likely for dissolution or "misplacement."

Let me give you a specific example. Say that a handkerchief was given to you with great love by someone whom you
no longer care for. The handkerchief is lovely, quite service-
able, almost new, yet not precisely to your taste. The relationship in question has cooled to the point where its memory
occasions no regret, only boredom and impatience. In your
view, the subjective reality of the handkerchief is diminished; its emotional "water level" is quite low. And so, in your
constant but unconscious mapping of your surrounding terrain,
you are no longer apt to see it as a reservoir of available
emotion. Mentally, you cross it off the list of things to which
you devote preservational energy. Like an untended pond, it
"dries up" entirely—but can reappear at any moment if
given a new infusion of emotional "water."

I am rather proud of that last analogy, for in it, I suggest
that like a pool or lake, an object is *itself* a field in which
further manifestations are possible. You can have snowflakes
within a cloud, or chunks of ice within a lake. So, in your
world, can a house or love affair manifest and then generate
still other "events" and condensations within its given field.

Again, all this is subject to energy. Because the intricacies
of energy-manipulation are so very complex, the majority of
them are left to unconscious scrutiny—for the unconscious
can keep things in better "perspective" than can the conscious
mind. So when you lose something, and when it comes back
to you or creates itself out of nothing, look upon it as a
dream symbol—as an object whose emotional reality does
not quite fill it from side to side; whose significance and
vividness are, as far as you are concerned, diminished. It
is neither hot nor cold, salty nor sweet, and so you tend to
spit it out of your reality.

This is a healthy gesture, for you all know people who
grasp to themselves the most insipid of friendships, fearful
that no new loves will build themselves up from the
ever-present surrounding fields. These individuals trek
through life like hikers trudging beside a mountain stream
with canteens filled with stale and tepid water bouncing
at their sides.

It is not vital to trust me on this next point, but vital to
trust *yourself* that if you need and desire to have certain

objects and events manifested, you will quite unconsciously find yourself in the right place at the right time. You do not find icicles in August or snowballs in July—generally. But regardless of the season, if you have genuine need of either one, do not be surprised to find yourself in a refrigeration plant where a local field overrides the general one, where the usual rules are suspended. To the degree that any object or event is a condensation of a larger field, to that degree it *is* an exception to the general rule! Realize that you are all glorious exceptions to the apparent "rule" of non-being and unconsciousness, and you may feel freer to violate the rules and "likelihoods" and no longer shackle your happiness to the law of averages or your fulfillment to the limits of probability.

You will let your river overflow its banks—or rather, *be* in the river during that once-in-a-hundred-years when it chooses to do so. Understand that wholly unlikely events are most emphatically *real*—that their lack of plausibility does not reduce their concrete reality one iota. Then you are well on the way to grasping how the slippery but quite necessary quantum physics of your own mind creates the world you know.

Some teachers say that creating wealth is our natural birthright. Then why do so many people remain poor?

Many of you hobble your capacity for financial enrichment —for a number of reasons. Identify your fears and anxieties in this regard, and it will be far easier to *allow* the influx of material comforts that is indeed your birthright when you take on physical form.

If any of my readers believe that money is not a "spiritual" topic, then it is precisely for those readers I am speaking. The more you squirm and feel uncomfortable about material wealth, the more I encourage you to read on!

You will agree that the well-to-do can become "better rounded" than those whose resources are severely limited. Yet your culture has evolved the most profound mistrust of abundance. In your James Bond movies, the villain is a man of fabulous wealth, as if that were circumstantial evidence to be held against him. In your novels and even children's stories, the wealthy are often morally primitive, using their resources to magnify selves not worthy of such magnification. If Man is inherently sinful, then better that he remain poor, lest he have disposable income to lavish on heroin or booze—or on guns, bombs, and armaments.

The belief that money *must* corrupt is often a form of sour grapes, by which those of meager resources can rationalize their relative poverty—but that is as discriminatory and self-delusive as any other bigotry. That which you denigrate in others, you effectively banish from your private experience—and that includes wealth. Not that riches by themselves produce saints and mahatmas, but poverty stunts more characters than it builds. One who lacks sufficient resources to participate in society feels more or less disenfranchised, excluded from the general banquet you all incarnated in order to attend. Your society suspects that while the "filthy rich" may be corrupt, those with no funds at all are merely filthy—and thus, beneath consideration. It has been many centuries since beggars have been suspected of being Zeus or Christ in disguise, but not too many decades since wealth was perceived as a sign of divine favor. It behooves you to understand the reasons behind this change of heart, for wherever riches are suspect, poverty will remain a problem.

An amusing myth many of you share is that affluence does not descend until late in life. And so, you lump the advantages of wealth together with what you perceive as the *dis*-advantages of old age. You can see this irrational equation in comedies: Wealth is concentrated in the hands of those "with one foot in the grave and the other three in the cash register," as Thornton Wilder put it. If you hold that belief, you are certainly going to see increased income as hazardous to your health.

Another hurdle to prosperity is fear of responsibility. Each of my readers knows individuals who triumphed in one way or another and then, fearing that such dizzying success could never be repeated, slunk away from the arenas of their achievement. Yet many of your best triumphs are *given* you as part of the bargain you entered into by taking on flesh—perks, you might say, that go with being human. Thus, you may find money in the street, or be granted an uncommonly faithful friend, or discover yourself in "lucky" or "adventitious" circumstances.

Much of that which you need most—such as the legs upon which you stand, and the hands you use to make your way in the world—you cannot earn, but *must* be given. You did not earn the eyes you use to read these pages; yet none of you, even in the presence of the blind, feels guilty for being sighted. Those with particularly keen sight are not resented, nor envied. Nor do you feel that vision renders you susceptible to temptations such as ostentatious jewelry and pornography. Yet if only the rich could see, if the poor were left to exist in dim and groping obscurity, it would be a world strangely familiar to the one you know—for you often ignore objects you know you cannot afford. If you can barely pay your rent, you toss aside the Financial and Travel sections of the newspaper. Even if earning a decent living, you are apt to be "blind" to those on a separate economic stratum. You do not ordinarily strike up conversation with panhandlers; neither do you wave into the tinted windows of stretch limousines.

Now, for those who suspect I was a Marxist in several of my lives, let me explain it is not money that divides your society into rigid classes, but your *perception* of money's effect upon the personality. As myth would have it, one needs good taste and refinement to spend money wisely—yet one must lack compassion and sensitivity in order to earn it in the first place! You misperceive millionaires as hoarders who hide goodies away from a public who could otherwise enjoy them—a prejudice that hardly reflects the realities of financial life. Anyone who succeeds in his or her own area of achievement is by definition a conduit, a fountain, an enabler who permits *others* to fulfill themselves to a superior degree.

An individual involved in real estate once requested the dubious pleasure of speaking with me face-to-face. I advised this gentleman to look at himself not as an entrepreneur but as a servant—whose role was to find for others the homes and offices in which they could best fulfill their private purpose. He was to view himself as a matchmaker, contributing to the betterment of those whose unconscious wisdom led them to his office door. And that same prescription will be equally healthy for anyone who desires material *and* creative success in any field whatsoever.

If you see yourself as a competitor in the corporate jungle, you issue a silent but effective challenge to those programmed to accept such challenges. If you see your chosen field as a place of cutthroat competition, then you effectively *demand* contact with those who have your worst interests at heart. If, on the other hand, you see yourself as an *effective* enabler who seeks to make life better for all who enter your influence, then you automatically align yourself with well-disposed colleagues and devoted customers. I am emphatically *not* advocating a Pollyanna attitude in which wishful thinking substitutes for intelligence and common sense. Success depends on acute empathy and identification with those around you: You must feel their frustrations as your own! Then, in seeking to enable and dis-encumber them, you automatically reap the benefits of your altruistic creativity.

By "creativity," I mean the versatile, spontaneous imagining of new solutions to problems that others have treated with received wisdom. If many of your millionaires seem eccentric, it is because success means seeing the world through one's unique vision and politely testing standard advice against one's own intuition. The millionaire was eccentric to *begin* with, daring to think his fellow men might appreciate a more economical motor car, a vaccine for a dread disease, or a device to speed their work. Even if his inspiration was not dramatically visible, nonetheless it created some new avenue where there was none before.

Yes, simply by imagining abundance, you can bring it about. But such pre-imagined riches will not "take" unless you feel comfortable with them on an emotional level. *Unless abundance feels appropriate to you, and unless you feel thoroughly entitled to it*, then your psyche will seek to cast it off, even as your immune system eliminates proteins that it decrees are foreign to the body.

If you are lonely, you can imagine a lover to your liking. You can even precise-ify that individual's exact characteristics and trust the universe to honor your request. But if you have doubts about romance or suspect the opposite sex is out to take advantage of you, then no amount of "creative" imagery will improve your social life! Similarly, for those who seek to acquire—and keep!—enough to live on gracefully, I suggest the following exercise:

Take some time alone. Imagine, in as complete detail as you can, a typical day in your life—into which additional prosperity has flowed. Except for that leap in income, the day is normal and ordinary in all respects.

Begin with yourself awakening in the morning, under new sheets and in more comfortable pajamas than you presently wear. Breakfast on fresh-ground coffee and nourishing fruits that now you pass up as too expensive. Continue on thus, throughout your day until—again, in your imagination—you retire for bed.

Along the way—and this is one of the crucial aspects of this exercise—be alert for any moments or situations in which you feel guilty or ill at ease. Do you sense you are overindulging yourself, perhaps at the expense of others? It is wise to write down these incidents and examine them at some length, for they represent strong aversions—sore spots of the conscience, you might say—which thoughts of abundance tend to irritate.

In imagining your affluent day, it is important to envision any new items you have purchased as broken in and accustomed to, *already* part and parcel of your life. Do not imagine yourself wearing brand-new shoes that pinch, driving a car whose gleaming finish requires polish every morning, or faced with rich delicacies that make you break your diet. But if you *do* imagine such unpleasant drawbacks to wealth, *write them down!* These are the literal representations of fears and assumptions—beliefs, in other words—that you hold about wealth.

If you perform this exercise correctly, proceeding through your *entire* normal day and leaving nothing out, you will see how your "private" affluence inevitably spills over into the lives of others. As you move into your daydream life, invite as many others as you can to join in your good fortune! You can share your imagined abundance in any number of ways: bringing home fresh flowers for your spouse, sending your children to a better school, or arranging a vacation for a parent or close friend. Recognize that your extra income has been spent most wisely—by encouraging those who offer superior merchandise and maintain high standards of quality, taste, and craftsmanship. Your extra income enables them to provide first-rate goods and services available to an even wider range of customers.

Quite literally, most of what you enjoy—the home in which you live, the clothes you wear, the food upon your table—was made available to you by the affluent. A poverty-stricken grocer would have very disagreeable stock indeed! A builder forced to cut corners could not create dwellings in which you would care to live.

It comes as a surprise when those especially favored in any way—extraordinarily good looking, talented in one of the arts, possessed of charming personality or great spiritual wisdom—gently accept their bounty, being neither falsely humble and self-deprecating, nor arrogant and boastful. It is more surprising still that most of these gifted, gilded individuals consider themselves the equals of their fellow men and are *more* literally "citizens of the world" than others perhaps not so conspicuously favored. Their advantages bring them into closer contact with their surroundings! Able to pay their phone bills, they can talk to more people at greater distances than the individual who must husband every dime.

Contrary to the Scrooge image, then, *wealth does not isolate you.* Rather, it opens countless new avenues of rewarding communication with others who share your interests and enthusiasms.

Money is *not* power, but rather, an extension or automatic byproduct of ability. It comes most easily and quickly when one is fully engaged in one's chosen activities. Those who use it most joyously do not consider it a distraction, but rather plow back the profits into the business—and that "business" can be children, painting, gardening, education, or whatever. If you see money as the life-blood that enables your society not only to exist but to *perform*, you may feel more comfortable about it. View yourself as its temporary custodian or trustee, using your best judgment as to how it may effectively be spent. Then you should have fewer qualms about its corrupting influence —and thus, come by it more easily.

In this way are riches integrated—welcomed unconsciously and without reservation—into the whole of an individual's life. And thus are men and women released into the full achievement of their lifelong goals.

PART TWO

Who

You

Really

Are

4

Triumphal Entries into Flesh, and the Springboards of Congenital Choice

• Miscarriage and abortion • Choice of gender and sexual preference: why individuals choose in advance to be homosexual • Significance of the natal chart in astrology • Why ESP is highly developed in children • Acne and adolescence • How the physical body reflects the inter-face of spirit and personality • Mental components of illness, addiction, and overweight • Sudden physical changes • Rejuvenation by suggestion • Maximizing one's life span

If natural miscarriages can result from a mother's change of mind about having children, isn't abortion a violation of sorts?

Any event that you decide to participate in is a matter of choice. And choices *will* be made, one way or the other. Basically, the problem with abortion—and it *is* a problem—is one of conflicting desires: mixed signals on the part of the mother. If she truly wanted a child, she would behave in one way; if she truly did *not*, she would behave in another. Instead, being tired of the ambiguity of her own feelings, she chooses situations that will force her hand.

I know, I am answering the question in a different way than you posed it. However, as you—as a society and as individuals—learn to precise-ify your desires and intents, the question and issue of abortion will become irrelevant.

No form of life conceives unless it wishes to, unless there is an unconscious choice. Where is your awareness? Where is your focus, your concentration—your consciousness? Do you believe that your body is going to foul up unless you keep a close watch on it? To what degree do you wish to let your body make its own choices? Do you want to make choices *for* your body?

These are the real questions. All of them underlie your issue of abortion, which is merely the tip of the iceberg. If you want to resolve the issue, look at your conflicting belief systems dealing with your own bodies, and the female body specifically.

As far as abortion is concerned, you cannot make choices for others. However, you can say, "In my house, on my block, on my street, this shall not be an issue!" You can form your own mini-societies in which abortion is not necessary, for you will have used your own awareness to insure that it does not need to be.

Starting with yourselves, there can be a snowball effect. And when enough of you are aware of your own body consciousness and that portion of it that welcomes other entities into physical life, then for you and your immediate neighbors, abortion will no longer be necessary, or even desirable.

And so the issue will come to rest: not through legislation, but through *ability*.

If our Oversouls are androgynous, why do we have biological genders—as we know them—in this world?

For one reason, it is more fun that way! Gender is yet another means of precise-ifying or focusing in on certain aspects of your total nature—with which you need to make contact or need to explore. If you were playing a chess game, you would sit down to focus yourself on the board. And when you captured a pawn, only your hand would bother to move.

Gender is an accepted way—biologically and socially—of focusing, but so is physical reality itself! For example, you decide which side of the street to walk on—in the sun or the shade, depending on the temperature, your own inclinations and, of course, on where you want to go shopping. But next time you come downtown, the sun may have shifted, and your priorities may walk the other side of the street. You always have to focus—a source of never-ending delight and a choice that can indeed be changed between lives.

Why do certain individuals choose to be born gay?

You could just as well ask why certain individuals have a sweet tooth, or easily learn to play the piano, or are adept in athletics. Predisposition toward one's own gender is a form of focus—an area of specialization, if you will—in which certain goals may be accomplished much more easily.

The underlying "reasons" derive from motives that originate in the inter-life state; so it is pointless to go searching for physical or psychological "causes" for homosexuality, any more than you could reduce all tastes and inclinations to a matter of enzymes or childhood upbringing. There are a *number* of these motives, which should come as no surprise if you notice the wide variety of attitudes and lifestyles within your gay (and non-gay) communities.

One of the most popular is the lure of exploring sexual attraction with the brakes off. Most so-called courtship behavior is an attempt to mediate between the quite different needs of the male and female of the species. By pairing with one's own gender, one amplifies the traits of that gender. And in many ways, it is easier to "come to grips" with one's own gender by a close emotional involvement with that same gender than by seeing one's actions reflected in the sometimes distorting mirror of the opposite sex. Many heterosexual sex symbols do not really understand the source of their appeal, but few gays do not know their balance sheet, you might say, down to the last item.

Another motivation is the avoidance of children as a consequence of physical intimacy. Many gay people are active in modes of creativity that demand quite a bit of free time— into which the responsibilities of raising a family would bite rather deeply. And may I say, without trying to be smug, that this is one area where Freud's equation of art and sublimated sexuality breaks down completely? There are healthy people of all sexual persuasions who do not wish to be hauled down to a child's level except on *their* terms, and who find one or another means of remaining childless. This, then, is not one of the chief "reasons" for being gay, though it is usually paired with one of the other main ones—as an added attraction.

Yet another challenge that being gay affords is the romantic position of rebel, misfit, "me-against-the world" outcast. The role of the one who does not fit in is age-old and has been filled by hermits and holy fools, inventors and stage actors, artists and prospectors—to say nothing of less reputable individuals such as Robin Hood and Billy the Kid. By being gay, you can enjoy the paradox of being physically beautiful and socially adroit and yet, out of step with a society that you perceive (of course!) as dull, stifling, and unimaginative.

Whether you choose to live that role with panache and style, or play the wounded victim of an uncaring and bigoted world is up to you entirely. Throughout your history, gay people who were the most egregious rebels against their societies have been laid to rest with laurel crowns and highest honors. No man or woman has ever been persecuted *solely* because of his or her homosexuality. Being gay is quite literally a handle on the world, and like any such handle, others may use it conveniently as a means to handle *you.*

Among women, now, the motive for being gay is more a desire for understanding—for being understood—than for sex *per se.* In many parts of your culture, women are made to feel as a minority; and gay women are able to savor the "minority" experience in undiluted form.

With men, another common motivation is one of self-enforced restlessness. In another life, the soul may be slothful or lethargic, allowing itself to sink into what it perceives as a rut—now, it has chosen a societal role that demands an extra measure of vigilance, alertness, and observation. Being gay means never quite relaxing and letting go, but always keeping one ear cocked for the undercurrent, the subtle meaning, the hint below the obvious. Those who "were" bored with a placid, stolid, straightforward life will often choose to be gay the "next" time. And it is no coincidence that so many gay people congregate in cities where the overall pace, energy, and stimulation *aside from sex* are at their peak.

Any form of focus is a sort of insurance policy, meant to restrict the self to areas of experience where it may most fully expand and most swiftly learn. Just as with any form of insurance, the underlying motive is a form of fear. Not that gays are more timid than their straight counterparts. As a general group, they think things through, weigh possibilities to a finer degree, and are more willing to make calculated sacrifices than those who have chosen a sexual orthodoxy that, in some ways, is not nearly as easy to satisfy.

One's astrological birth chart has been described as the blueprint of one's soul. Could you comment?

Indeed I can. A natal chart is a bit like a chess problem, in which your beginning position determines how you will play. Rather than start the game neutrally, with rooks, pawns, and knights in their traditional places on the board, you array them in "conjunction" or "opposition" to one another, so that they can exert challenges of different sorts.

Your astrological birth chart is not as deterministic as you may have heard. Rather, it is a symbolic statement of the "game plan" you have chosen for yourself. But you want to use a diving board as something to propel you, not restrict you.

A typical Gemini or an archetypal Capricorn has, in a sense, chosen to play from his or her natal power base. But like a chess piece, even they can move to a different square! If others do not at all fit the astrological pattern, the astrologers say, "Ah, this person was not born at the stated time," or "One planet must have been overlooked when the chart was first drawn up."

You are not bound or "ruled" by your natal birth chart. It is more of an opportunity. But because opportunities are usually grasped, you take advantage of it. Because the positions of the planets at your birth do give a certain emphasis, you are more likely to run with these existing energies than you are to rebel needlessly.

Does knowing a person's zodiac sign help us understand them?

It is indeed possible to classify individuals according to zodiac type and other astrological parameters. Were you to cram all your Libras into one room, however, you would find enormous diversity among them. You would also find that some "official" Scorpios would, during certain months and seasons, behave precisely like those of other sun signs!

The reason is not only because of different planets in the charts but, because as you go down the corridors of life, every so often you put out your hand to steady yourself. In any one life, your total configuration of behavior will be a bit eccentric, disobeying some of the rules that you came into life obeying. If you say, "I am *only* a Leo and, therefore, cannot partake of the other signs and their abilities," you are selling yourself short.

If you say, "I always have to live up to the potential of my sun sign," then you *also* sell yourself short. Every so often, you need the wonderful ability to fail, to let others down when they over-depend on you. That letdown can also be in terms of expectation, for you deeply disappoint others when you fail to be predictable by obeying the rules! If people say you are a double this or a triple that, with your elbow conjuncting your solar plexus, and you refuse to behave accordingly, you can expect to see many long faces!

A delightful young lady, not present tonight, was not pleased to hear me say that spring flowers *obey* the seasons. I took it back and said they *take advantage of* the changing weather. Similarly, you take advantage of certain emanations of the zodiac. Those of you branded Aquarians or Capricorns partake more easily of certain attributes and vibratory patterns that are, however, available to all. You are not *obeying* as much as utilizing certain "energy enzymes" of the universe.

It is rare, but by no means unknown, for an individual to become ill from the effects of the planets. You will eventually be able to chart a correlation between those who have unexpected or unforeseen health crises, specifically of the endocrine system, and astrological conjunctions. Conjunctions do not cause such breakdowns as much as a form of vibratory "malnutrition," which in turn brings on the enzyme or hormone imbalance.

If you are tall or blond, or play the violin or sail on Chesapeake Bay, you can take advantage of that classification. And as long as you do not become *bound* by your classification, nor use it to bind others, then you will be doing very well indeed.

Why do so many young people suffer from acne?

Eruptions of the skin are largely a result of aggression that is not expressed emotionally or physically. The general rage and rebellion that erupt in many young people cannot be wholly discharged. The results show themselves forth on those parts of the body most accessible to sight.

Not that emotions can miraculously materialize themselves as pustules and acne. Rather, the anger these young people feel is turned against the self and builds up within the system any number of hormones and enzymes that, unless worked off through exercise of the skeletal muscles, tend to be secreted through the pores. You can appreciate that a hormone that acts in a stimulating way upon the human system can well have a similar effect upon bacteria naturally present in the skin.

You have not fully explored the means by which emotions affect the body. Hormones like adrenaline are responsible for many physiological changes, but emotion can also affect the cells directly, causing them to secrete within themselves whatever enzyme or hormone is called for. Thus, many of your endocrine glands are more or less coordinating organs, and the hormones they release modulate—stimulate to a certain point, and no further—secretions produced by many of the body's individual cells.

If the muscles had to wait for adrenaline to reach them through the bloodstream, quick reactions would hardly be possible. Instead, individual cells pick up from the body aura the fact of an emergency and hasten to produce their activity-inducing substances. The adrenaline later "endorses" their decision and helps transfer such substances out of the cells and into the bloodstream where they can be disposed of.

Your scientists already know that individual cells can produce interferon on their own, quite independently of the immune system—a prime example of the process I am talking about. Many, many other such enabling substances are produced by individual cells. Your doctors have not detected them because the vast majority of these chemicals are designed to break down quickly, lest they overstimulate or injure cells in which they originate. By the time blood is sampled, the only chemicals measurable are analogous substances secreted by various organs. The original "fire extinguisher" has been totally used up by the time the fire engine arrives.

Physical exercise and sexual activity both help burn up the aggression-chemicals that result in acne, which is why many teenage myths have a core of truth to them. Again, the basic cause of acne is not anger or aggression *alone*, but that such impulses are blocked or suppressed and not allowed to expend themselves in physical activity. Running, to speed up the metabolism, would be of just as much use as soap and water; and the use of a sauna and large quantities of ingested water to induce heavy sweating would be of as much service as the various ointments used to curb bacteria on the skin surface.

What are some of the reasons behind addiction?

Many of your psychologists agree that addiction, to drugs and alcohol in particular, causes a pleasant narrowing of disagreeable stimuli. While under artificial sedation, the body literally "feels no pain," and the mind of the individual is chemically focused on the here-and-now. There is no grieving over lost opportunities, no worries about the morrow. In a very real sense, the intoxicated person enjoys the same present-tense euphoria experienced by those adept in meditation. And if the chemical ladder to serenity is a bit more shaky and dangerous, it is also rather more dependably *there*—no training whatever is necessary to achieve a 100-proof satori!

You may point to other addictions, such as tobacco. Again, the main asset of any addiction is that it narrows choices. If one is used to scattering one's energies—well, then, the hunt for heroin or a fresh pack of cigarettes can focus those energies to an amazing degree. Thus in a sense, addiction provides meaning: One's entire life falls into obedient orbit around the dark star of the substance to be sought. And this feeling of direction, of a discipline imposed from without, often sets off intimations of security in certain childish layers of the psyche.

This is why so many addictions are hard to break: In a very real sense, addicts are asked to bid goodbye to a stern, exacting, but also quite rewarding behavior pattern with which they have become intimately acquainted—and onto which they have allegorized any number of parental attributes. To break the habit, addicts must go through a kind of psychological puberty in which independence, however cold and lonely, is seen as preferable to continued bondage to chemical apron strings.

Do those same principles apply to overeating? Can you explain why—even though some people are born with a genetic predisposition to obesity—our culture discriminates against fat people? And how can we effect long-term weight reduction without damaging our health?

One reason why the overweight are looked down upon in your culture is because on an unconscious level, excess body weight is rightly perceived as a form of avoidance. The overweight individual frequently adopts extra poundage as a means of rendering him- or herself unattractive sexually and thus, "out of danger." Note that the bias against fat *women* is somewhat more pronounced than against fat men: By her weight, the woman is basically saying no to all comers. This peremptory refusal is reacted to as a form of hostility.

Of course, there are other meanings to overweight. Some who associate rounded contours with babyhood, adopt excess weight as a badge of innocence. Others, perhaps with unconscious memory of adjacent lives, see overweight as a status symbol. In time past, when food-gathering took up much of the day and meals were shared on a tribal basis, only the elite were granted extra portions and allowed to become obese. As recently as your 19th century, overweight was equated with success in business, and the ability to eat—and by implication, pay for—vast quantities of food was considered a mark of status. So, today, those who are overweight but not *truly* affluent can be perceived as pretentious, adopting a symbol to which, strictly, they have no right. The hostility that arises is perhaps mingled with the suspicion that these individuals are taking more than their share of available foodstuffs.

The Japanese expect a sumo wrestler to be heftier than the norm. So the *circumstances* of the extra ingestion are taken into account and weighed in the balance, as it were. And because other values from tribal times are by no means dead, you will notice that the construction worker or head of the household who has attained his girth from eating and drinking among his fellow workers or at family celebrations is rarely censured— welcomed, in fact; whereas the solitary eater who has "sneaked off" to eat "stolen" food in private tends to be shunned.

Yet another basis for bias is the recognition that overweight is not healthy for the body that must support it. You are instinctively programmed to shun members of your species who have something wrong with them—a rather uncompassionate but effective means of preventing the spread of contagious diseases. And you do perceive—if unconsciously—the circulatory and metabolic burdens under which an overweight person labors. More recently, this basic aversion has broadened to include social behavior. Thus the "weirdo" is shunned, even though he or she be in perfect physical health. And should an overweight person have attained that state through psychological imbalance, that will also be perceived unconsciously and added to the individual's demerits in the community.

It does the obese no good to declare that they do not subscribe to the tyranny of fashion, that they defy the dictum that everyone should be slim and willowy. Simply by choosing to live within a given community, you implicitly agree to recognize its laws, standards, and customs—and any who claim to pick and choose which standards they will obey are seen as self-deceptive, at least to some degree.

Overweight, then, can be as much a means of belonging as a form of rebellion. Should your circle of friends be overweight "rebels," you are not likely to disappoint them with great success at dieting. In many communities, extra poundage among the middle-aged is actually a gesture of modesty: "I do not wish to be slimmer than—and therefore compete with—my friends." Not that the overweight seek each other out; rather, their mind-sets tend to reinforce one another, and their overweight is a product of their value system.

One can also add extra poundage as insurance: against the hard knocks that might injure a leaner frame; as a means of adding bulk and substance to an ego perceived as too spindly; or as a means of hoarding against expected loss. For who can take away from you what you have beneath your skin?

It is unfortunate that most of your diets stress denial, for this signals a warning to the body consciousness that food is in short supply—which of course encourages the storage of *more* fat, not less. Indeed, the rapid weight gain that often follows a diet is the body's instinctive preparation for the next "lean season" of dieting! The best way to diet—or rather, eat sensibly and effectively—is to sit down to meals with the sincere belief and affirmation that you can eat all you wish. And by truly eating no more than you *want*, your weight will sooner or later dip to its optimum healthy level.

The trick here, if trick it is, is to reassure your body consciousness that food is so very abundant that it is quite redundant to store up any fat within your cells—not when there are fruits and meats, condiments and pastries in such abundance in any corner grocery, to be had practically for the asking. Thus, if you project your larder *outside* of yourself and assure yourself that you will never be denied access to it, then it is much easier to become finicky about food—to improve your eating habits by looking on fish, lean meats, and vegetables as status symbols, or by teaching yourself gourmet cooking. You want to become discriminating in your gastronomic tastes, so that you spend as long selecting a desired meal as shopping for a new wardrobe.

I'm attracted to the vegetarian ideal and wonder if eating only fruits and nuts would supply all my nutritional needs.

Yes and no. It would be difficult to eat *only* fruits and nuts for one's entire life and still maintain a healthy regimen of incoming nutrients. Certain substances are seldom present in vegetable matter, and a great deal of what you eat requires catalysts or enzymes within the body—and not just within the stomach, either—in order that the body may make use of it. In the wild, herbivores eat rotten fruit and leaves in great quantity—thereby ingesting quite a bit of insect matter and bacteria which serve as a kind of terrestrial plankton, supplying many of the trace nutrients they need. The relatively cosmetic, sanitized produce of your modern-day farms and markets is often too much of a piece and, not being ragged around the edges, does not allow "outside" nutrients to seep in. A *very* wide variety of herbs, including many of those traditionally used for healing and folk medicine, dried and taken as a tea, would be a fine supplement to any vegetarian diet.

It is wrong to blame those who gorge or "pig out" occasionally—*occasionally*, now—for in so doing, they are effectively topping off the batteries or filling the reservoir that cleans the windshield. Every so often, your body senses the lack of a certain nutrient and assures it gets what it wants by creating a craving for an appropriate foodstuff. Pregnant mothers are notorious for this kind of gustatory intuition.

How you think of food determines to an overwhelming degree how your body will make use of it. Thus, anyone who enters a dietary regimen with reservations or doubts is likely to encounter malnutrition—which may be subtle indeed, but malnutrition nonetheless. Just as the body needs a wide spectrum of vitamins, proteins, and minerals, so does the psyche require *experience* to nourish it. You are best nourished when your meals are served under a variety of circumstances, and in different company now and then. In this light, the practices of eating out, gourmet cooking, and backyard barbecues make better sense.

I am not endorsing binge eating, much less the vomiting up of food shortly thereafter, for binge eating would be far less common *if the food were retained* and allowed to satisfy the need for which it was originally ingested. Rest assured that any food-desire allowed to *truly* satisfy itself will quickly evaporate. So, I encourage you to discover exactly what foods satisfy your craving best—which is your body's way of trying to guide you to what it requires.

What beliefs and attitudes lie at the root of problems with eyesight—specifically nearsightedness and farsightedness?

Your operative beliefs are about perception vis-à-vis wisdom—to what degree do you subscribe to them?

Many of you see a "farsighted" individual as one of superior grey matter, who knows not only when to get in out of the rain, but when to buy Polaroid stock. In your society, an individual must be old, grey-haired, and venerable to have amassed such wisdom. Do you still wonder why the elderly are farsighted?

You tell your children, "See what's in front of your face. Be aware of the obvious!" So, the nearsighted person often prefers to focus on individualized details. But a focusing of intent results in a change of vision, so it is normal for near-sightedness to correct itself automatically as you grow older.

The best way to cure vision problems is to focus on that which is lovely. Even with glasses on, your eyes and your spirit will reach out and wish to see more. If you are farsighted, a flower, butterfly, or crystal will tempt your eyes to look more closely; if you are nearsighted, a sunset or distant mountain. Your core beliefs are not always in your head—they are all around you, personalized and physical-ized. Sometimes, you may find them reflected far more powerfully outside than within.

I'm not a professional athlete, but still I have chronic knee pain. Can you tell me why?

In Western culture especially, the knees bear a heavy symbolic burden, being the "organs" of prayer, obedience, and submission. Anyone who has problems with authority figures, who bridles at the thought of kneeling to another; who has been frustrated and impatient with the dictates of organized religion, *especially as administered by a parent*, is going to be prone to knee injury or pain in that joint—pain that will resolve itself when conflicts dealing with "giving in" and submission are resolved.

Long-lasting pain is nearly always the psyche speaking through the body consciousness, asking that a long-standing but contradictory belief system be resolved or "straightened out." In essence, long-term pain results from the personality wanting something both ways—by not wholly rejecting what it seems to abhor. The obvious result is a double-bind situation in which the body is checked in its own innate efforts to balance itself.

For centuries, but especially since psychosomatic medicine told you it was normal to do so, you have been using your poor bodies as dumping grounds for unresolved wastes of the psyche. Each of you takes things that are too much for you to cope with, emotionally or mentally, and you say, "All right, body, take care of it!" And so, you get a headache or a racing heart or—no pun intended—cold feet.

Like a guilty corporation, you dump your personal "toxic problems" where you *think* you will never find them again. And you have your own private and collective symbolisms for parts of the body. Therefore, when a body part gives out or is injured, it is quite often because you—in your own mind—have declared that part of your body off-limits because of psychological problems "dumped" on that site. Those of you who have trouble with your ears are often not pleased with what you have been hearing. "This organ," you say, "stands for something I do not approve of. So it may suffer injury as the whipping boy for conflicts that I cannot experience emotionally."

If you have physical problems, first see what the afflicted part stands for as a symbol *for you.* You do not need a textbook to tell you what a given body part signifies; its private associations will immediately leap to mind. Next, look at the affliction as if it were a dream symbol, and your body itself were a dream—which, in certain terms, it is. From my point of view, our friend here is a dream body I have created so that I may enter your collective 20th-century dream.

Illness, in those terms, is a bit like a nightmare. But as you know, you ascribe nightmares to something arising from your unconscious psyche. And physical illness is no different from a bad dream: Both are symbolic expressions of that which the psyche has chosen *not* to process.

Your ultimate way toward health is to make a pact with your body. Promise never to give it anything it is not capable of handling; that your emotions and psyche will *themselves* handle anything they can *best* handle. And ask your body to give back to you anything that you, in ignorance, have dumped upon it.

After you make such a request, your next three days may be the worst of your life! But you will not be given back anything you cannot handle; and indeed, your body *cannot* handle your emotional hangups, your problems at work, or your problems with your brother-in-law. Do not ask your body to be a prime minister or a psychoanalyst. Your mind was created to handle those problems. And so, give to your emotions and to your intellect the problems they are equipped to handle! Let your body do what it does best—feel the breeze on its face, smell the flowers, and digest big bags of french fries. Let your body do—joyously, energetically, and enthusiastically—what it was created to do, what you allowed it to do when you came into this life. And let your mind take care of its own hassles—as it will, if you allow it to.

My mental energy varies a great deal. Sometimes I can sail through the day; other times, I catch myself daydreaming. Is there any way of bypassing those times, so that I can be clear and focused whenever I want?

Even your washing machine must go through a rinse cycle, you know! If you think you must control your thinking apparatus, you are turning one of your greatest sources of inner nourishment into a mechanistic system.

Many of you have risked what you call "health challenges" because you have tried to control your body, coercing this incarnate colleague of yours to do your society's bidding. You would not want to inhale without ceasing—you would eventually explode! There are times for ingestion, digestion, and elimination. Some stages are more intriguing than others, but all have their necessary place. You should not confuse one stage with the other, nor assume that any stage is going to be eternal.

It's not so much when you *want* to be clear and focused as when you *need* to. Sooner or later, an infant begins to sleep and eat on a regular basis, because the wise parent has let Baby eat and sleep as it wants, on demand. Your body and psyche will find their own proper rhythms, but if you are constantly jostling them, it is very hard for them to develop their own beat.

You have enough schedules! Trust yourself that you will perform—mentally, emotionally, and psychically—when you need to and will then develop a proper rhythm. When you find yourself fantasizing, it will be a familiar "time" to do so, and you will be wholly engaged in the process. You will not be marking time, looking at your watch, tapping your foot for the next stage to begin—for only *then* are you wasting your time!

*Recently I met a man I haven't seen since we were boys and was
shocked at the changes in him. After we parted, I felt grateful
for not having wound up like him—not a very commendable attitude, I suppose. Yet ever since, I've found myself growing more
confident, compassionate, and loving. Is there any connection?*

Yes. During periods of personal growth and evolution, you
will often meet acquaintances out of the past—who have changed
drastically, often for the worse, and leave you happy to be quit
of them.

In effect, what you do at such times is hold a psychic house-
cleaning, trotting out superfluous and outgrown aspects of your
personality and, in a sense, paying old acquaintances to cart
away the discards. Thus, you feel revulsion and pity at the same
time—revulsion, to see your previously hidden shortcomings
in full daylight; pity that another should take up what you
now know to be valueless and counter-productive.

It may seem unfortunate that people, apparently to expiate
their karma or simply out of habit, choose to become incarnate
replicas of the Aztec Filth-Eater, who devoured men's sins much
as ants and beetles are used to clean skulls in medical labora-
tories. Such individuals are often disabled in some way—
by accident, by precarious health, by some disfigurement
of the mind or spirit. Yet, by collecting negativity into themselves, they perform a useful function that has its just reward
on a higher level. They set free such beings as strive for
better things, and take upon themselves the restricting rags
that others might not have been able to cast off.

You can look upon your old friend, then, much as you would
upon a garbage collector: with pity that he must endure the
smells and stenches, and gratitude that the ziggurat of rubble at
your curbside, dug from the dark basement of your soul and
rank with memories of disappointment and spoiled possibilities, has been so neatly cleared away.

This is another instance of how apparent evil, lust, and
squalor can actually operate to a higher purpose. When a
group or individual wishes to improve and ennoble itself,
another individual or group may suffer apparent degradation.
Recall the parable of the devils whom Jesus cast out: They
entered a herd of swine, who flung themselves into the sea

to be drowned. How kindly, do you think, must God smile upon that host of sodden little piglets? For they were sacrificial, just as Jesus was prepared to be.

It is a high—no pun intended—feat to handle filth and not be the least corrupted by it. But that is what the Christ story illustrates at its deepest heart: that one *can* deal with filth and still come out smelling like a rose.

After beginning a love affair, I noticed a startling changes in my posture—even in the bones of my face. Can psychological changes bring about such distinct physical alterations? And will our relationship help ensure my good health?

It is entirely normal for you to change the configurations of your physical body—or "being," as you think of it. However, it is not usual to redecorate an apartment all by yourself. First, you would call your roommate and say, "Okay, what would you like to have here?" Your new decor becomes a collaboration with the individual who is there to share and enjoy it.

Not that any bodily changes must be endorsed, seconded, or approved by another, but they are more easily attained when someone else is there to approve you—or goad you on. Just as you might not buy a pair of shoes until someone else says, "Yes, they look good on you," so you might not be willing to complete a given bodily change until it has a proper audience.

Alone, you will make other changes that you would *not* make in another's presence. You deliberately run certain experimental programs on your bodies—both in health and non-health, I might add—because you do not want the consequences to be judged by others. You want to be your own judge.

To the degree that each of you can be sharers and private judges of your own body, to that degree you will be recipients of perfect health. You must say, "My body is my ambassador in physical existence. It need not always answer the desires, wishes, and protocols of those around me, but at the same time, it must not cause them—or me—affront or embarrassment."

You must encourage your body to be a diplomat on its own time, not merely a child who is constantly being told, "Now bow. Now curtsy. Now shake hands." The body must be allowed to grow up on its own, even though in your terms, strictly speaking, the body is finite and mortal whereas the "wiser" soul is not. Yet the body consciousness, the true ruler of your body, is immortal and cannot be dismissed as temporary—as too many of you have.

Similarly, it is too easy to say, "My particular relationship with my body will die when I do—when death do us part." I tell you, rather, that what you *learn* in that relationship continues. Today, right now, you are learning what you will need to be healthy the next time you take a canter through physical existence.

And so, in a sense, does the relationship with your body consciousness itself continue after death, even as a correspondence may continue on, even if the individual letter-writers relocate themselves on your physical globe. The letters may arrive with different stamps and postmarks in different-colored inks —yet their correspondence continues.

Could one use mental exercises to create thicker hair, whiter teeth, and unwrinkled and unblemished skin?

One could indeed, but the variable is *your* motive for desiring those fine and comely attributes!

If you desire good looks merely to increase your personal power and seductivity, then portions of your Grander Self are going to contest the point, perhaps to bring you to a finer balance of self-acceptance. Your highest challenge is to be good at being *whatever* age you are. If you believe you can be in perfect health at every age, then beauty and other attributes will all take care of themselves, following in the wake of that core belief.

Appearance alone is no criterion of health. Rather, health produces good looks as a *byproduct* of itself. By "health," I mean that graceful and attuned state of mind and spirit that has often been called grace—although traditionally, grace is bestowed by some higher power. In fact, grace is a latent, innate attribute of *every* living thing and needs to be released, not beseeched.

Even if your creative exercises were not wholly successful in *this* existence, they might well influence the bodies you choose in some adjacent lives. In many cases, disfigurements and "unfortunate" physical attributes are a form of inoculation, you might say, against such shortcomings in adjacent lives. Someone may choose a withered arm or baldness in one existence simply to achieve great strength or a full mane of hair in another. Athletes often back up before rushing forward to take their leaps, and so will the Larger Entity sometimes—*sometimes*, now—seem to empty its lungs of breath in one incarnation that it may fill them all the more deeply in another. The more purposes a given attribute serves—and that includes illnesses and chronic "complaints" that you may have been seeking to rid yourself of—the easier you will find it to achieve or to maintain. Thus, white teeth had better be good for chewing! Thick hair must not be used to decoy others into believing you are twenty years younger.

It is not wise to divide the nation of your body into so many provinces—skin, teeth, hair, lips, muscles, eyes—to be governed separately by different rules. Health is too often impeded or blocked by such extreme specializations—and by comparison to the health and appearances of others, which is even worse.

Individual wellness manifests itself *throughout* the body. Not that you should neglect brushing your teeth and combing your hair, but such actions are finishing touches to the essential first step of ministering to your body so that it may achieve its *own* version of perfection, not necessarily one that mirrors a starlet or fashion model.

I'm less afraid of dying, really, than of living in pain. Yet I can't seem to get rid of unhealthy behavior patterns. How can I become more confident about my health and longevity?

It does not matter so much how *long* you live as how *well* you live—no new thought to anyone familiar with Classical philosophy. I would add that what you see as "unhealthy" behavior patterns may, in fact, be ways of letting off steam —bleeding off anxiety and negative energies that, if allowed to remain, would be far more detrimental to you.

Look around, and you will notice abundant examples of individuals whose enjoyed behavior, though somewhat excessive, does them no apparent harm. Sadly, you can also find plentiful individuals who—for example—smoke, knowing it is bad for them. Such people are basically hypnotizing themselves in a negative manner, accelerating whatever unhealthy effects they suffer. Others view certain inescapable "facts" of daily experience—exposure to sun, air pollution, everyday stress —as highly unhealthy; and thus greatly increase the malign effects of those stimuli they interpret as "bad."

To ensure good health, anchor yourself imaginatively to a hale and hearty future. Specifically, envision yourself in old age as a spry, agile, limber, and glowingly radiant human being. Imagine yourself bounding out of bed. Create, if you will, a few ailments—bursitis, minor arthritis, perhaps a cataract— from which your body has recovered, resoundingly and to the astonished approval of your doctors.

Envision, further, that whatever undesirable genetic tendencies you may have inherited have been de-activated—had their fuses pulled and their tubes crimped shut, you might say—so that there are no latent health hassles lying in wait, ready to explode as you turn the corner of age 89.

A specific example: It is common knowledge that the vast majority of old men in your culture develop a pre-cancerous condition of the prostate gland. Note, however, that the majority do not suffer prostate cancer! Being subject to a condition does not mean it need affect you in the least! And do not let statistics rule your life, any more than you would feel compelled to vote along with the majority on an issue when you strongly held a minority view.

Simply by maintaining your health and "proving that it can be done," you enable others to resonate to your example. Conversely, do not allow yourself to resonate to others— especially members of your family and close friends—who are sickly or in poor physical condition. Compassion and identification are too easily linked and confused in your culture. Just as a scientist must not contaminate himself with the disease-causing microbes he investigates, so must you operate according to a different set of "rules" than do your brethren who do not remain healthy . . . and I suggest that these rules have less to do with taking vitamins and avoiding anxiety than they do with visualizing yourself as in the pink of health, regardless of the warnings, forebodings, and predictions of your all-too-readily quoted medical establishment.

I am not advocating denial of any sort. Rather, I suggest you insist on the limitless powers of your body to repair damage and forge solutions to whatever assaults physical reality may mount. Recognize and root for the winner! Of course check your brakes and wear your seat belt—but recognize, too, that many people have walked away from car crashes with nary a scratch. There are countless reports of spontaneous remissions of even the most dread diseases, including AIDS. Allow yourself the sneaky, rebellious fun of being one of these lucky, healthy mavericks!

What's the maximum life expectancy that we can attain?

Is a long day in summer necessarily better than one in winter? When you go to your art museums, do you measure the size of each painting? "Here is a Renoir—but this Braque is longer!"

Is a glorious, enjoyable, healthy, happy, productive life, seemingly snuffed out at 52, a tragedy? Would you prefer that same individual survive to 120 and *really* get on everybody's nerves? Longevity is a tape measure that unfortunately stretches in only one direction. With it, you cannot measure achievement, love, compassion, wisdom, or understanding.

I am not advising you to run out and play in the traffic! But remember, this present moment is where you are living. If you are not living *now*, then you might as well be dead—because *then* you will be alive indeed! That is why many of you die: for greater life and awareness, for greater wisdom and compassion, to say nothing of other attributes.

When the bus you are riding upon has come to its stop, only then do you get off. If you have been going to the gym and taking your vitamins, you will step off that bus a very healthy individual. But step off you will, because you know —as any wise, intelligent individual knows—when it's time to get off, in more ways than one. Pun intended!

5

Evil as Inability

• Dealing with boredom and repetition • The origin of fears, and how to "whittle" them away • Dynamics of mental illness • How your beliefs can improve your reality • Fostering and expanding creativity • The proper use of ego and preconceptions

Many of your theologians have postulated that evil is a separate force in the world, opposed to the good and in basic balance with it. Still other philosophers have suggested that evil is simply the *absence* of good, and thus cannot exist in an entirely good universe—and needs no more than a simple dusting-off of the good in order to vanish entirely, as darkness is dispelled by light. Yet those who have fought in battle, sought to overcome sickness, or put themselves into uniform to keep peace on your streets can attest that evil seems to be stubborn and persistent, with an active life of its own.

And so, the apparent paradox: Does evil have an independent existence? If not, did God create disease and war—and the cruelty that so undeniably thrives in the hearts of so many? And if evil is *not* inherent in Man, then why should you have to suffer for it at the hands of evil-doers? In dealing with such dilemmas, your thinkers are more eager to look up one another's opinions than they are to confront their own private experience. It is fortunate that you cannot learn to walk or digest, grow or love, by reading how to do so in a book, for were such knowledge available, you would have no need of incarnation at all!

I am not denying the value of the printed word. But unless you perceive books—and essays such as this—as mere springboards, mere introductions, to your own daily experience, then you have missed their true value. You must judge according to your *own* heart, and use none but your own understanding in weighing the balances that your colleagues force into your hands.

I wish to enlarge the scope of our discussion by citing what every parent knows. At birth, a child cannot speak, sit up, or grasp an object for more than a few seconds. In an adult of 25, such helplessness would be deemed a tragedy, but in the infant, such lack of skills is seen as entirely normal. And so, parents take enormous pride in a youngster whose drooling, crying, and toilet habits would be a source of acute embarrassment ten or twenty years later.

I have just given you the key to evaluating evil, and also to how it comes about: *Evil equals inability.* High time we spun off from that basic theorem a few corollaries that may help your exploration and understanding of everyday life!

The newborn of our example has no easy task ahead of it. It must learn to do all those things its parents can—ideally, more! Worse, it must attempt the vast majority of these tasks by trial and error, so that many toys must be broken and many limbs bruised before these adult skills are attained. The trials of childhood are, you might say, "necessary evils," but they are *transitory*—agreed to and willingly shouldered as temporary, as means to a greater end.

A wise child is not terribly afraid to be wrong, to realize that its world view must be dismantled. The blocks set up on the rug to form a grand cathedral must be taken down and put away before suppertime. Looking to those who are older, taller, and wiser, the child realizes instinctively that it will not always be young, tiny, and ignorant. The evidence and promise of growth are all around! And so, the child is steeped in an evolutionary imperative, while those around it measure its monthly growth and applaud the acquisition and mastery of even the simplest new skills.

But what if this challenge is denied—either by the child or by those who care for it? The decision to reside in a state of *permanent* inability is the source of the worst evils of your world.

As just one example, your psychologists point out that many mental afflictions are the result of arrested development: The child does not progress beyond a certain stage physically or mentally, sexually or morally, and does not enter the postpubertal "promised land" of ability and accomplishment that is its by right. When a child "sits tight" or reverts to an earlier, "safe" means of coping or behavior, *then* what you define as evil comes about.

It is similarly unwise if any being, at whatever level of attainment, decides to rest on its laurels and keep on with business as usual. Your adult universe may not be as explicit a schoolroom as it was when you were a child, yet it is still most emphatically a place for continual learning.

Not only is evil the same as inability, but *inability too is relative!* To the degree to which you refuse to grow and evolve, to that degree you become a tribulation to those who must put up with your behavior. But once you have learned to do anything properly, you no longer need cause damage, offense, nor obstruct anyone else's fulfillment—until your colleagues progress to your level of attainment, and a bit beyond.

All of your myths illustrate this point quite well. Satan, as your theologians have it, was *incapable* of accepting the love of God and, because he *could not* enjoy Heaven except by becoming top dog thereof, was cast down. One amusing—to me, at least—detail of your devil-myth is Satan's quite unbelievable stubbornness: He is wholly *unable* to progress beyond a level of resentment and revenge that even a ten-year-old would find babyish—indeed, quite tiresome.

To me, it is significant that you often equate evil with bestiality; that those who are "possessed" traditionally display the behaviors and noises of beasts. Yet on the other hand, you assign some of your own noblest attributes to animals: courage to the lion, loftiness of spirit to the eagle, loyalty to the dog, gentleness to the lamb. Of course you can have it both ways, but be aware that those bestial qualities you view as negative—in yourself or in the animal kingdom—are supposedly *fixed*, whereas the more praiseworthy attributes are not desirable simply for themselves, but are basically means to an end. That is, loyalty by itself is rather pointless; one must have something or someone to be loyal *to*. Every one of your traditionally sanctioned virtues is basically a template for correct behavior. Context is seldom provided: You can simply fill in the blanks, because one virtue should fit all possible situations—and one soldier's courage seems indistinguishable from any other's.

On the other hand, cruelty, vice, destruction, animosity, and revenge are *not* prescribed behavior—and thus, quite creative in their expression. Since no book teaches you the "rules" of evil, you must figure them out for yourself and strike out on your own. Pun intended!

Now, I have just handed back to you one of your own misconceptions. You can see that by our earlier definition, "good" demands a far wider range of skills and a more thorough effort at self-expression than does evil. Your greatest humanitarians and creative geniuses have been completely themselves, expressing their talents and good will in a most individualistic, even idiosyncratic, manner. The problem, of course, is that it is far easier to fall back on those skills you have already perfected— to break a door open, say, rather than learn to be a locksmith. But whenever you opt for the easy way out, you not only delay your own development, but usually damage some delicate mechanism in the process.

I will try to hurdle one of the basic paradoxes that prevents you from perceiving good and evil to be what they really are.

Some of your theologians claim that evil is necessary, so that Man may better understand good by comparison. Arrant nonsense! Not one of you needs to feel pain in order to experience pleasure to the fullest. Were evil a necessary foil or contrast to the good, it would need do no more than lurk in the wings, as it were, providing a certain suspense and apprehension to heighten the appreciation of the good being played out on stage. Instead, evil makes quite dramatic "entrances" into your personal world in the form of invading armies, disease, muggers, vermin, and what-have-you. It seems propelled from within, under its own steam—and thus, theologians try to conceive of how God could have allowed such monstrosities to come into being.

It would be a cruel God indeed who created nothing but babies who knew how to smash watches. But All That Is allows babies to grow up and become watchmakers, so perhaps the universe is not so cruel after all! In your spiritual and chronological development, you pass through any number of unpleasant or downright repulsive stages. But these passages are not to be mistaken for, much less welcomed as, permanent estates.

To return to our parent-child analogy: The *experienced* mother knows that the "terrible twos" are a stage that her child will soon outgrow. The physician knows that sooner or later, the fever breaks and the vomiting passes away. The weatherman knows that no matter how hard the hurricane may blow, calm and blue sky must return.

I want to emphasize that evil, as you commonly define it, is an unhappy instance of arrested development, of whatever sort. A great many contagious but benign micro-organisms have evolved out of species that in your not-so-distant past used to cause plagues and suffering of the worst possible kind. An organism that causes disease has not yet found its equilibrium with its host. Similarly, any individual who must compete, overwhelm, and do damage to fulfil his desires has not evolved far enough to be able to satisfy those same desires—as well as even more rarefied ambitions—in concert and cooperation with others.

To put it succinctly, evil is *always* relative and exists for no other purpose than to make you long for something better. In other words, evil's innate "purpose" is not served if the evil-doer cannot abandon it as a poor deal. Neither is its purpose served if you, the evil-sufferer, cannot get out of the way in time.

Now, of course, my readers will asking *how* they may avoid evil! And though my answer seems simplistic, it is anything but: I advise you not to play its game.

Your Bible says, "Resist not evil." Most parents know how to ignore the child who is being an annoyance—but the *wiser* parent knows that ignoring a child is the surest way to create a little monster whose behavior is far worse. The trick is to calmly refuse to accept the terms which an apparent evil-doer presents to you.

The evil-doer usually stabs, robs, lies, or inflicts pain because these methods demonstrably *work.* Because he is good at these skills, he continues to practice them—yet realizes that these skills *are* limited and, consciously or otherwise, longs for a wider range of personal accomplishment. Now, certain of your personal-safety experts have advised a woman walking alone at night to *approach* a suspicious man and ask if he would please escort her safely to her door! This works because of its appeal to the growth ambition in all consciousness, including that of a would-be mugger.

This is why mobs have such a sinister reputation: They reinforce in their individual members the lowest common denominator of skills and behaviors which obviously work—and which, all too often, include violence. Members of a mob mistakenly think that surrendering to a mass consciousness will somehow empower them far beyond their individual abilities. To a point, it will, but only by—to use an analogy—using a larger hammer and exerting a harder blow. And so, the joys of marching or rioting always pale next to the *individual* sense of breakthrough and achievement. Private success can always be replayed one way or another, but it is not so convenient to find a mob properly riled up and willing to go along with your desire of the moment.

The child will keep trying to ride a bicycle, no matter how many falls and skinned knees transpire. Mountain climbers and yogis will endure what to most of you would seem like severe pain. The urge to better one's present level of ability is age-old, innate, and is *the* single most potent antidote to what you see as evil in the world, whether of the transitory or the entrenched, seemingly long-term kind.

But those who try to grow can seldom do so in the presence of others without making themselves mildly ridiculous. When the baby stumbles and sits down suddenly, visitors laugh. When the member of a teenage gang betrays kindness or an interest in the world's finer things, he is hooted at and made to feel out of place—which of course he is! There is no more out-of-place individual than the mountain climber, the deep-sea explorer, or the student struggling to master a new language.

With this discussion behind us, I think it will be far easier for you to understand why malefactors and "Satanic" forces so often portray themselves as reptiles, fanged mammals, and other creatures that display unambiguous power. Rattlesnakes do not negotiate or, at least, do not need to. And of course, the snake has demonstrably traded inability of a sort—being limbless—for the advantages of being able to coil its body, strike, and pass through very narrow spaces. In short, the snake is an emblem of evil because its means of communication appear so limited (if you are a mammal, that is); because it has deliberately thrown away what you most dearly want to preserve; and because it is for the most part solitary, quiet, and unsmiling. It is not like a caterpillar, which undergoes wormlike servitude only that it may emerge resplendent with velvet wings that delight the human spirit. No, the snake's only apparent ambition in life is to swallow other creatures and grow to be capable of swallowing ever-larger creatures. A better image of the wantonly *un*able and hence "evil" human personality could hardly be imagined.

There is no *necessity* for skinned knees. But if you are going to learn to walk, much less grow to adulthood, bruises are going to be so very likely as to *seem* inevitable. Because so few of you are endowed with beginner's luck, you are likely to encounter evil or inability in one form or another, in yourselves or your colleagues. *But as long as you perceive such "evil" as an implicit stimulus, as a call to more sophisticated action of one sort or another, there is no way it can do you lasting damage.*

Astrologers hold that a planet going retrograde is a bad omen. Just so, the dog returning to his vomit, the so-called backslider, the recidivist criminal are seen as especially disreputable—because the power of the familiar has, however temporarily, overcome their instinct to conquer new inner territory and master new techniques of living.

And so, if you would avoid evil both in yourself and in your world, I give you a single admonition: evolve! Or rather—because you *will* evolve, inevitably—I bid you embrace your personal evolution with the arms that Evolution Herself provided you with.

The teacher who keeps a child in school on a brilliant fall afternoon may, to that child, seem to be the personification of ogrehood. So *any* slight, hardship, or injury may better be viewed as an encapsulated learning experience. You can always learn *something*, if only not to beat your head against the brick wall that has dazed and bloodied your colleagues. You can learn by their mistakes as much as by your own, and the more inabilities you can identify in others *without condemning them, and with the deepest and most sincere compassion*, the less so-called "evil" you will find it "necessary" to undergo.

I hate going to work to face the same old problems. What can I do to make life interesting and exciting—even when it has to be boring and repetitive?

Please note how cleverly you have boxed in your options, with the qualification that life *must* be repetitious!

Quite often, work *perceived* as boring and repetitive is not a symptom of the workplace, but the byproduct of the worker's own belief system. In such a case, you have allegorized certain virtues onto repetitive, predictable routine: You view recurrent phenomena as basically reliable and dependable—hence, praiseworthy. You asked that there shall always be food on the table, yet did not stop to wonder,"What if it's the exact same menu every time the dinner gong peals—morning, noon, and night?"

You *do* have natural cycles, after all—of the sun and moon, of inner glands and outer gears, by which you and your associates can set your clocks and plan your times together. Yet it is too easy to view what should be a spiral—a three-dimensional structure—in terms of two dimensions: namely, as an endless circle. While the spiral keeps you within a comfortable circumference at all times, yet it extends you outward; but a circle merely returns you to your *exact* point of departure. It protects, but does not challenge.

Now, just as the Earth describes a spiral in its passage through space, so does *any* job, no matter how routine, seek to thrust its workers into the future—to evolve itself and them together. However, your desire for stability and regularity—perhaps devoutly wished for back during a time of job change, divorce, or moving—may, years later, find a suitable ground in which to flourish, and send down strangling roots. Prayers *are* usually answered, but sometimes not for years after the initial request. If you ask for a pair of long pants, say, you may get them only after your legs have stopped growing.

Almost inevitably, someone who has come to worship the sane virtues of permanence—preservation, tradition, nostalgia, the old-fashioned way, *maintaining* good health, *keeping* fit, *staying* young—will grow a crust of boredom and rigidity to protect against vicissitudes, which are seen as threatening.

To change these rather depressing circumstances, you need only open your mental shutters to the breezes of change—to the opportunities for vast and sweeping but welcome changes, in your place of business and personal life.

Winds can cleanse and freshen and not merely put your desk into further disarray. Career changes and new personnel are as vital to a large organization as the circulation of blood is to the body, and for precisely the same reasons. Understand, also, that any corporate body undergoes periods of dormancy before springing into a new, sometimes awesomely sudden period of growth or transmutation. And simply by being *aware* that such changes are imminent, you will then perceive their first stirrings and portents and will discover new cracks and creaks, new signs and developments that your co-workers ignore. That alone should result in ceaseless fascination.

Without change and development, you would still be on the low side of puberty, if not a one-celled organism with neither limbs nor lungs. And in light of your body's ultimate but necessary dissolution, it hardly behooves you to grip so tightly the play money printed for you to joyously squander in those few hours before the carnival is over.

Why do some individuals scatter their energies so much that they can't accomplish anything?

For the same reason that some men flirt with every pretty girl at a party, or why some play as many lottery tickets as they can.

In a child's view, all parts of the universe are equally fascinating: If one is not in as many places as possible, one is sure to miss something. This is why childhood often seems so frustrating, and explains the eternal popularity of the three-ring circus—a rather accurate model of how a child suspects the universe must really be. Later, however, the adult learns that what has once been missed will inevitably come round again, and that one can accumulate almost as much by waiting as by frantic pursuit.

But along the way between childhood and maturity are those who do not trust the universe's natural abundance, who have no faith that what they need in life will seek *them* out. And so, they revert to a childish mode: By trying to cover the bases and play every number on the roulette table, they hope to increase their chances of winning.

Their actions also express an inner fear of having wasted one's time on a project that proves fruitless. And so, like a walker on thin ice who spreads out his weight as widely as possible, or like an overly conservative investor who diversifies his portfolio into every conceivable field, such individuals agree to pass up sizable rewards in exchange for no greater risk. Fear of disappointment, of *loss*, is their overriding concern.

It goes without saying that such energy-scatterers become easily bored and have short attention spans. They have learned to taste the essence of things quickly, and do not need to penetrate deeply to satisfy their curiosity. They are fast learners, and have a basic mistrust or skepticism toward anything slow and painstaking, such as law or government. In a sense, they are children of the morning of life, having preserved within themselves the attitude of distracted-but-happy bewilderment that characterizes the infant.

I am not necessarily endorsing their approach. Just as some adults revert to childish mannerisms by way of defense—"I am acting like a child; therefore, treat me with the compassion you would use if I were one"—so do others revert to childish *methods*. Again, this arises from fear that opportunities will be missed.

In the animal kingdom, fear results in any number of distorted and unattractive behavior patterns, all adopted for the sake of defense. The sea cucumber vomits out its entrails, grasshoppers drool brown saliva, mammals cringe and urinate. And it is much the same with humankind: Wherever fear is, there comes a corresponding loss of dignity and abdication of one's inward purpose.

Can you explain how the emotion of fear originated?

Fear, originally, was a signal that one should back off and not get involved until one had more developed skills for handling that given situation. Fear ensured that a young animal—or human—could survive without the mother or father constantly monitoring every decision that the child wished to make.

At its healthiest level, fear is a message that tells you to defer a given challenge or exercise until you are older, wiser, or more accomplished—which time may be only a few minutes hence, or may even be right now! It is worth listening quite carefully to what the fear *has to teach you.* Once its "lesson" has been learned, you come away with a new resolve—and, eventually, new skills you can employ to overcome the challenge that once you found so fearsome.

Chronic fear, then, is a form of internal nagging: You are being reminded, again and again, that a previous challenge of your development has not been faced squarely. You resist it not so much because of the *original* fear as out of a sense that —because the fear-message has been repeated throughout your life—you are perhaps incompetent to counteract the fear-stimulus.

There is no one who is, or *should* be, fearless. But healthy individuals shed fears the same way they discard dead skin cells or hairs, or scrub off the mud adhering to their hands after a productive day in the garden.

Whenever you fear anything, you are in a sense identifying with your adversary—which you see as more powerful than you. You are a society—I did not say "race" or "species"—that believes in playing imaginative games, much as when your Pentagon asks, "What will the Russians do next?" The mother cat who defends her kittens feels little fear indeed, for she does not stop to identify with whatever is threatening them. To do so would scatter her energies—and she is single-minded upon the defense of her kittens.

So if you wish to be fearless, start by learning precisely who and what *you* are, and who and what *you* want to be. Security lies only in ability, but you cannot begin to develop those abilities that are uniquely your own until you allow the Divine Itch to show you where to begin scratching.

I have a number of mild but irrational fears. Is there any simple method of doing away with them?

If you fear anything, try whittling, which is very simply this: Ask yourself, "What is so terrible about that?"

As an example, someone we once spoke with was in dread of contracting rabies. And we asked him, "What is wrong with a fatal disease?"

"It would kill me," he said.

"Oh?" we replied. "What is so bad about dying?"

"Nothing," he said, "for I have to die sooner or later."

"Well, then," we asked, by way of further whittling, "what *are* you afraid of? The pain?"

"No, but the pain might make me cry."

"And what is wrong with crying?"

Finally, our friend discovered his root fear was of appearing weak in front of his wife—a fear that he was able to handle quite efficiently, once he knew it for what it was. His fear of disease had been huge, but by whittling away at it, he reduced it to its true dimensions—and revealed its true identity.

Now, imagine that you are groping in a pitch-dark room, and see a tiny ray of light coming through the wall. You reach for your pocket knife and begin whittling the aperture. Still more light floods. Soon you can see where the door is—and you are free. So it is when you whittle at the things you love. Rather than diminishing, their inner virtues will expand and become clearer, both to guide your way and to give you additional options—openings, doorways, windows, paths you had never hitherto suspected.

Start with things that attract you in the physical world— what you admire most and love most in life. Then ask, "What is so *wonderful* about that?" Sooner or later, you will find yourself saying, "Well, it's not just the puppy I love, it's his affection, his trust, his total commitment."

Your intent—or rather, the intent or "shopping list" of your Grander Self—will soon make itself very obvious. For if you look at your shopping list at the grocery and see upon it "Eggs, flour, baking soda," you know that your intent, your mission, is to bake a cake. Whereas if it is "Vodka, gin, rum, and vermouth," you're going to have a cocktail party.

Your built-in tastes—what you are most apt to respond to —comprise your shopping list, which is given to guide you through the aisles of physical life and show you what to take down off the shelves—and yes, what to leave there!

You must precise-ify your desires: That is negative and positive whittling, in a nutshell.

Why do some people seek fame? And why are there groupies who want to hang around famous people?

The desire to attain fame or to experience it by association has its roots in the quest for identity.

Those who stand outside in the cold imagine that being within the walls of a house—*any* house—must be paradise itself. So do those with shaky concepts of identity and self-worth view fame as the panacea for all their problems. The media does a very good job of precise-ifying the images and personalities of those it profiles. You have at your disposal interviews, photo essays, and recordings in which the famous present their idiosyncratic views of life. And it seems that the more idiosyncratic a personality, the greater the media attention. Thus, it is too easy to assume that public notoriety will somehow absolve one from making up one's mind about what to do with one's life—and what image to present to the world.

This trap explains why so many groupies are younger adolescents trying to find their niche in life. It explains, too, why those who attain fame early in life often later experience great pain and confusion, for their own media-image hardens around them, preventing further growth. Thus, many of your adult celebrities act in rebellious ways that would seem excessive even for a reform school dropout—and reporters again and again shake their heads as to why so-and-so, who had everything going for him, chose to end his life in such wretched fashion. More than one of your actors has chosen to be murdered at a fairly young age so as to escape the possibilities of *self*-destruction.

Not that celebrity invariably produces spiritual emptiness. Rather, it throws into deeper and more agonizing relief whatever spiritual poverty there may be. To revert to our first analogy, the warm house is not necessarily a place of tranquility, but you cannot tell that simply by gazing in at the glow cast by the fire. Nor do the distinctive garments of your rock stars, or the three-piece suits of politicians, necessarily ease them through the day.

*My daughter has developed some channeling ability, but she
questions it constantly, asking, "Am I a bit nuts?" If the information she gets is useful and valid, does it really matter
where it comes from?*

It matters, if you are worried about the label—"GUCCI" or
"MADE IN JAPAN." But if you only want a vase in which to
put your flowers, does it matter whether the vase be Ming,
Lalique, or a plastic container? If you plug in your television
set before dawn, you get a test pattern. Later, once you get
your set adjusted, you may indeed watch costume dramas,
Julia Child, or anything you desire. Channeling usually begins
like that: Once you have the means of receiving channeled information, you may want to fine-tune those same abilities so
that you can receive more and better "programs."

You quoted your daughter as having asked, "Maybe I'm a
little crazy?" I would like to put in a word of affirmation for
what you consider to be mental illness. When cameramen do
zoom shots, they often have to *de*focus on what they were
focused on. You see this in your best movies: For a moment,
the lens twists out of focus to perceive an important figure
at the back of the room. From my point of view, your "mental
illness" is nothing more than taking a little longer than normal
—in your terms—to focus again on a new object, or new area
of intent.

So, when you see one who questions her channeling, or
one whom others claim is a little crackers, understand that
these people are readjusting their equipment. If you sit down
before the symphony begins and do not realize that the musi-
cians are tuning their instruments, you will wonder why you paid
so dearly for your seat—is *this* the noise you are going to hear
all evening?

Those of you who re-tune your mental equipment also produce some bizarre "test patterns." If you want to see such people in their true glory, you must be patient.

*If we create our own reality, why do circumstances often seem
so stubborn, so resistant to our efforts to change them?*

The outer world is . . . okay, this takes a bit of explanation.

The inner psyche is quite capable of rapid change and self-
transformation, but is accustomed to making such changes only
in response to external stimuli. If you believe that circumstances
are hopeless, then your psyche is effectively forbidden from
seeking out changeable areas and "weak spots" on which it
might seize and exert pressure.

"If I cannot influence the world," the discouraged person
thinks, "at least I can have dominion over my own being." And
so, the change-making impulses are turned inward, even though
both body and mind are remarkably refractory to sudden and
arbitrary changes.

Let me clarify that: Great changes in the psyche are of
course common, but are built up to slowly and prepared for with
exquisite care and efficiency. Any "overnight" change may
have been months or even years in coming, just as a flower bud
that opens in an hour may have formed the previous summer.
And so, the individual who is depressed—or more likely, bored
—with his lot will not find it easy to swerve the momentum
his life has accumulated up to that instant. He will not be
able to effect an immediate change for the sake of change
—or at least, not a lasting one. Such is the fate of the weekend dieter or would-be smoke-ender: Old patterns of thought
and habit return all too swiftly.

Paradoxically, this should be a cause for rejoicing! If these
old patterns are so persistent, imagine how permanent your
new pattern will be, once you have given it the proper energy
and practice it for a requisite amount of time!

A sculptor working with wet plaster is heartened, not
saddened, by the rock-hard statue he worked on only the day
before: Its having set so firmly assures him that *this* day's
work can assume a similar permanence. But the discouraged
individual cannot see that a new-formed wish is still soft,
malleable, and not ready to take its place among—much less
be used as a battering ram against—the old thoughts and beliefs he may wish to get rid of.

I have done any number of mental exercises, including self-hypnosis. Why can't I change my beliefs?

Beliefs are not changed by treating them as heavy, monolithic slabs that must be pried up from one side or conjured away by exercises that seek to attack them by unorthodox means. A belief is best confronted *directly* and examined in such exhaustive detail that you begin to see exceptions to the rule you have set for yourself—which preferable exceptions you can then choose to follow, nurture, and raise into full-scale beliefs of your own.

If you *believe* that beliefs must be combatted with methodology other than thought, then you give those beliefs a power beyond the normal, and make them refractory to the very kind of thought that is most efficacious in changing them. It is very hard to abandon any paradigm that makes sense, which is why beliefs that seem to mirror your outward and inward worlds are so difficult to alter.

All you need do is seek out the exceptions: for every wall, the cracks. For every dam, the freshet of water. For every desert, the oases. If you pay more attention to these divine eccentricities, where the universe dares to defy your expectations—in short, if you *expect* to be surprised—then you will effectively lubricate your beliefs to the point where they can be "rotated" by ordinary conscious will power and desire.

Please note that desire and will power are not the same thing, and work far better in tandem than separately.

How can I best expand my artistic creativity and use it as the basis of a whole new career?

You limit your progress when you think of your art as something separate, set aside, which you must find time for and cultivate like a rare orchid—when, in short, you think of art and creativity as somehow less robust and "practical" than the nitty-gritty chores of your everyday life. Too often, art seems ephemeral and less than all-powerful because it will not happen by itself and thus, seems thoroughly under your control.

I should add that the one who asked this question has chosen to sculpt in hard stone: a particularly painstaking means of bringing beauty into being. Yet rocks do take on shapes without any mortal bidding them to do so! If you look for the roots of your art in the material you work with *and* in your own nature—if you can sense the creative impulse latent in your fingers and also the innate willingness-to-shape-itself that lies like an answering spark in the paper or clay, oil paint or alabaster—then you will make the essential connection you need.

You are already plugged in, but need to have more current, more "voltage," flowing for both your and your spectators' sakes. Imagine that artworks are fairly bursting into existence in their eagerness to be, and you need merely be present as a midwife at the birth—of the noblest and strongest offspring of the marriage between human skill and nature's innate form.

Take your cue as often as possible from your materials, so that they lend a "hand" in the color and form of what you work on. Art of any sort is a cooperative venture, and you do not want to break the spirit of whatever medium you work with so that it is entirely tamed and no longer recognizable for what it is. Rather, allow your materials to retain some of their original appearance, for artworks are best served when still slightly crunchy and not overcooked.

Once creativity flows joyously, spontaneously, and efficiently, your career will take care of itself. A career is to the individual as the playing field is to the athlete—something chosen according to the individual's ability and particular challenge. You do not have to force a career, and it is better that you do not. The right job will present itself automatically if you properly develop yourself to receive it.

Some teachers suggest that we should go beyond ego and become aware of our thoughts, without repressing them. Others maintain there is nothing wrong with ego, unless it's been limited or inflated by erroneous beliefs. Which do you recommend: ego or non-ego, belief systems or perception of reality with no preconceptions?

Your process of walking has been amusingly described as continually losing one's balance and finding it again in the nick of time. I also call your attention to crabs, lobsters, and other crustaceans who shed their shells repeatedly throughout their lives. Soon after such a shed, the new shell hardens and be-comes rigid—protecting the creature and enabling it to move about, until the creature's inward growth again causes it to cast off the shell it once put so much energy into creating.

So it is with your beliefs and your egos. They provide for you a necessary scaffolding for your observations, a necessary point of departure into events and circumstances. They are hin-drances only if you choose not to change them—as if a lobster tried to stay inside one exoskeleton for all its life; or if you tried to hop down the street on your right foot only, not will-ing to "give up" that foot and shift weight onto your left.

You easily see how an individual's beliefs change in the years between infancy and adolescence; yet no one doubts that the individual in question is the "same" person. It is harder for you to perceive that you moult your ego as often as sev-eral times a day, swiftly forming a "new" one to serve the par-ticular environment within which you find yourself.

Specifically, you adopt different egos in the presence of your employer, your spouse, your offspring, and when you are alone. As with the successive shells of a crab, your various egos all have the same general configuration, but are most emphatically different. Just as your feet are mirror images of one another, so do your various egos have their own psy-chological symmetry—and are *meant* to follow one another in fairly brisk succession. Therefore, see your ego and your beliefs as tools with which you can manipulate and man-euver through your reality—and which become restrictive only when you stubbornly insist on using only one of them, or on clinging to one that is ready to be replaced or supplanted.

6

Your True Being
and Abilities
in Your Present Body

*• The energy body's 300-foot diameter • Aura levels as
sensory organs • The intermediary mode, assumption,
and resonance • Dreams: messages from the center and
circumference of your being • Astral projection, dream
recall, and the drawbacks of lucid dreaming • How some
dreams, far from being precognitive, offer experiences
that you need not undergo in waking life • Visions,
precognitions, and selecting the realities you want • The
true nature of time, and how to perceive it as illusion*

*A couple of weeks ago, I was hooked up to some biofeedback
equipment, dropping through my usual levels of meditation,
when I started to pick up an intense low-voltage electrical
charge. My subjective feeling was that I was spherical and
somebody had hooked me up to jumper cables. My EEG, which
measures brain waves, was stable, but my Galvanic Skin Re-
sistance, which measures body arousal, was all over the place.*

Others in various meditative and relaxive states have experienced the same kind of tingling and "electrical charge."
Many of you, bored with identifying with only your physical
nature, are reprogramming your sensitivities to be automatically, gracefully, and efficiently in touch with your *entire* selves.
And so, I must explain to you not just your body, but your *self.*

Those of you who have problems getting into a too-small
dress or suit will blanch when I tell you that the diameter of
an average human being is approximately 300 feet! Fortunately,
it is not fleshy, but composed of layers of energy. You are
each like one of your Russian dolls, with one energy "body"
inside another.

You who have televisions with rabbit-ear antennae know that your movements can alter the picture from several feet away. Beyond that perimeter, you have other, subtler layers of sensory energy that can tell you when your baby is in trouble in another room, when someone is coming through the front gate. Just as the atmosphere around your planet attenuates as you move outward into space, so does your personal energy attenuate somewhat as it extends outward. But on the energy level, there is no distinction between substance and sensory organ: Wherever your aura extends, it reacts to whatever energies it encounters. Hence, you cannot walk down a crowded city street without a degree of discomfort.

As you move inward toward the physical body, layers are more energized. In your particular case, you wondered, "What if I go in the other direction? Shall I use the so-called depths of my being as a springboard to reach outward?" You deliberately clapped upon your inner eyes a pair of binoculars, deciding to sense with the outer layers of your being as if they were your more familiar physical skin. But since you seldom use these senses consciously, your normal waking consciousness wondered what was happening! Many of you will be doing this, whether in the dream state or awake. As children ready for the next stage of growth and development, you are eager to flex your muscles and surprise yourselves with your own abilities. "Extra-sensory" senses are in no way extra, but came with the standard model in which you are riding around now, so learn how to use them! But some require an extra "charge"—not in terms of finances but rather, of power or energy.

If you will look back upon your lives, all the stages of your development—going to school, puberty, graduation, marriage, your first house—had fearful moments. Very few of you would regret having taken those steps. So now, if you occasionally feel odd phenomena, there is no need for you to have aches or growing pains. Say to yourself, "Let me integrate my Larger Self—that which I know I am—with these new experiences. Let them become a natural part of my being." And then, you can measure exactly how far you have come.

You who are into physics know that radio disks placed around a valley can function like a single, vastly larger disk and pick up a larger spectrum of waves from distant galaxies.

So you, as individuals, can link up. When you meld your energies together and there is no conflict, more of you are "parallel" than are at cross purposes. And when you meld your 360-degree, 300-foot consciousnesses as a group, you can sense even more than you could individually.

I dreamed about a machine that could pick up emotions and events that had happened in a room and then play back selected videotapes of the past. Could such a device actually be built?

Such "videotapes" are a fairly accurate analogy for your so-called Akashic Records. Individuals often ask me why they can't become aware of something or other. My answer is that the sought-for information is often none of their business! What difference does it make to know who committed adultery with whom in the 16th century—except to provide a transitory thrill you could get more easily by watching *Dynasty* on the tube?

Notice that the machine in your dream was programmed to pick up *only* that which was of interest to the investigators. So you—as individual psychometric machines—pick up only what is *truly* important to you. As living Geiger counters, you can be very sensitive indeed; but to "tune" yourselves, you first must be more sensitive to your desires and your dislikes.

That is the flip side of precise-ifying your desires: precise-ifying your *dis*likes.

Do our energy layers pick up the reality of the world about us, or merely a translation?

This is not as easy to explain as you might suppose. Imagine that between a Rorschach blot and the perceiver there existed a third item—a separate and independent construction, created jointly by the perceiver of the blot and by the blot itself. The perceiver might well mistake this intermediary mode, as I like to call it, for the blot, not realizing that it is more or less a consensus—a drastic oversimplification—of the blot's true reality.

With this in mind, it may be easier to see the allegorical overlay of a presidential election—indeed, of any social or political issue presented to the public for prolonged scrutiny.

While a nuclear plant shutdown, a reactionary politician, and a public figure implicated in a tax imbroglio are all literally "real," they also create intermediary modes—creative allegories of themselves with which the public can grapple and, thereby, struggle with its own concepts of right and wrong, of acceptable and unacceptable behavior.

In a way, it's similar to computer usage. One makes a copy of the software and uses the backup disk exclusively, salting away the original software in a safe place. So with the intermediary mode: It provides a handy replica of reality—a disposable, easily replaceable toy upon which hungry young psyches can cut their teeth without doing any real damage.

This accounts for the disquieting sense of unreality you often experience when, intuitively, you sense that you are not in direct touch with the mass event—election, earthquake, high interest rates—that seems to be affecting you so directly. At such times, you are dealing with an intermediary mode. Possessing its own consciousness, it tends to form and deform itself in line with the preconceptions and passions you expend upon it.

This, of course, explains why a politician is often perceived so radically differently in the mass media once he or she leaves office. The politician has simply slipped off an old intermediary mode and created—or allowed to *have* created—a new one, "with the consent of the governed."

The intermediary mode is present even in interpersonal relationships. It fits far more tightly and accurately, of course, but is still there, serving as a form of automatic transmission between the individuals involved. It fits somewhat more "loosely" during a family gestalt event, such as birth or death—again accounting for the spacy unreality felt during such times.

Can we ever perceive reality directly, without the intermediary mode or some other buffer involved?

An analogy will help me explain: Imagine a snail in an aquarium on the sun porch of a suburban house. All That Is, you will concede, includes not only the snail, but the aquarium, the house, the suburb, and the surrounding universe.

Now, how is the universe—even if we limit it somewhat; how is suburbia—supposed to manifest itself to that snail?

The snail would be quite unable to experience suburbia in its entirety, even assuming it wanted to, when many humans do not!

Is not the eyeball that focuses light a buffer to reality? Is the filter that lets a camera see into deep shadow not a buffer? Buffers can clarify and focus in ways that are crucial to accurate perception. Standing at the center of a nuclear blast, you would experience the phenomenon *directly*, but I doubt it would truly satisfy your curiosity!

The intermediary mode is itself a form of sensory organ. Remember, you need the skin that separates you from a pussycat in order that you may feel the pussycat's fur.

There is a *form* of direct knowledge, which I call assumption—taking into one's self another's experience, emotions, or perceptions. But these are second-hand goods of a sort, having been digested and processed by a mind and scaled down to comprehensible terms. As one's capacity grows, so does the full spectrum of what one can encompass and assimilate. But it may be useful to deliberately limit one's perceptions in order to see more clearly what one *does* see. If one is truly curious and truly healthy, there is no such thing as excessive specialization. Sooner or later, the narrow hole one digs always breaks through into a cave of unforeseen wonders and delights.

You perceive everything through a lens—a camera's, or a telescope's, or your own. Whether that lens is corrective or distorting depends on your skill, and your intentions. And by skillful use of such a "buffer," you can see farther—by millions of light years, in fact. In such a case, the question of whether you are perceiving *directly* is rather moot. Paradoxically, the intermediary mode serves to eliminate distractions, to allow two or more entities to focus on the basic interaction between them—while it allows them to go their separate ways and devote themselves to *other* realities beyond their mutual interaction.

Analogy time: When two individuals make love, it would be tragic if their lungs were distracted from breathing or their hearts from beating. In fact, such bodily functions *do* suffer brief interruption during periods of exaltation, which might be vastly longer in duration were lovers trying to perceive each other *directly*. Instead, the intermediary mode functions much as a cell wall does on the microscopic level, keeping identities separate so that each may retain its integrity and continue its basic functions—physical and psychological—without potentially dangerous interruptions.

Think of the intermediary mode as the projecting corner of a cube where three sides meet. All three sides have their common boundary at this point, yet its reality—its angle—is formed by all of them. It is at least potentially active: You can scratch your back against a corner, but seldom against a flat surface. One side of the cube may have a series of pictures hanging on it; the second might have in it a row of windows; the third, a door—but that common corner does not infringe on the freedom of any single side. Yet at the same time, it does define where the three sides "fit" in the larger architecture of the structure of which they are parts.

Imagine, now, a wall between adjoining rooms, where a door or window in one room must open through into the other. Pounding or hammering on one side of the wall will be clearly heard on the other. This analogy corresponds to the experience of assumption, where experience is communicated directly between two more or less equal entities. Yet there is still an undeniable division between the two "rooms."

Why do we so often allegorize or project onto other people, rather than accepting them as they really are?

For one thing, the self that you "are" is in a state of constant becoming. To accept other entities as they truly are, you must not accept only their present attributes. You must also allow them to reveal no-matter-what from their pasts and grant them the freedom, or trust, to become whatever *they* choose to be in future.

Such trust—such a long leash—is very rare in your world. Therefore, most people take mental snapshots of one another, which allow them to easily recognize one another at later meetings. Just as most maps of three-dimensional terrain are necessarily flat, so does any mental conception introduce certain distortions in its striving for accuracy. Another factor is that what an individual represents or "stands for" varies drastically according to the other individuals he or she meets. A man might be a dentist to his patients, a cad to his wife, a father to his children, a loving son to his parents, and a good friend to his neighbor. He might also be a mysterious foreigner of undisputed brilliance to a dental symposium in Tokyo. And to students who read his textbook on jaw reconstruction, without ever meeting him, he will be a source of inspiration and knowledge of which they must grudgingly absorb as much as possible.

Now, how would you propose to accept this putative dentist as he really is?

In this context, allegorizing is an easy, usually painless way of setting up pre-fab beliefs—flimsy ones that can be torn down and rebuilt when necessary. With the outer world, you often tend to cast your beliefs in steel or at least, in fairly durable metal. But when it comes to other people, there is a general unconscious consensus among you that the beliefs—or allegories —must not be too tight or too stiff to prevent either perceiver or perceived from moving freely through their chosen roles.

Many instances of hate, prejudice, and violence in your culture arise when one individual swaddles another in a too-tight, too-restrictive mold that leaves this other no freedom. *True* freedom is simply the freedom to better one's self, to evolve, to show unexpected talents and goodness, and to become *ever* more capable—across the board. In a sense, then, beliefs are much like digestive enzymes within the body: They help you gain specific "nourishment" from your world and the other individuals in it.

In the body, certain enzymes are programmed to extract nutrients from one food and no other—which is why digestion takes place at different stages throughout the intestines. So with beliefs: Early in life, you may consider your mother to be your entire surrounding world. Later, she becomes an authority figure and finally, if you are fortunate, a friend and near-contemporary. If these various roles were mingled together, you could not appreciate an individual's different aspects in their own sweet purity.

A loving patient-dentist relationship is not only different from a loving man-woman relationship, it runs on wholly different rails. Different responsibilities are required of the various parties in each case. Just as an amorous dentist would not be the best candidate to perform root-canal work on his lady friend, so a man fascinated with the contours of his mistress's bicuspids would not make a very good lover. And so, *necessarily*, you narrow and restrict your focus, so that from any given relationship, you may draw nourishment in a fairly pure state.

Many individuals, in your species and others, prefer to sip their experience in small teaspoonfuls—that it may be more easily digested, and thus be more nourishing.

Is there a way of perceiving an animal from the animal's point of view? Katherine Kurz and other science-fiction writers have postulated a kind of telepathy in which one incarnate takes on the "memories" of another, and emotions and significances are shared—to such a degree that the sharer actually relives the other's experiences. Is this possible?

There is indeed a form of knowing more direct than can be obtained via the intermediary mode. I call it assumption.

Essentially, there are two ways in which an entity can take on, or assume, another's emotions, sensory experience, or even attributes. One is via the body's cells: Pain or trauma or, in rarer cases, ecstasy and actual sensory impulses can be transmitted across space—and, necessarily, across time—to jangle and stimulate the cells and, in particular, the nervous system of a second party. In the other form, which is vastly more common and cultivated on my level than on yours, the receiving "organ" for the stimuli is the entity's etheric body or non-physical essence. In your incarnate case, obviously, the two ways can overlap.

The problem with assumption, as you may have surmised, is one of assimilation: How does the receiving entity use sensory data it has assumed into itself? For to a startling extent, any creature self-edits and predigests what it perceives.

What a cat perceives may be entirely different from what you would find remotely interesting. Because that cat's perceptions are pre-coded—pre-sorted for delivery to specific sites in its nervous system—it might be quite difficult for you to process that cat's perceptions, much less make sense of them. To use a printer's term, they would be off-register from your own. They would not meld with *your* templates for incoming data, which would largely blur the feline impressions you hoped to receive.

But yes, inter-species eavesdropping is possible. One can tap into the sensory hookup of an animal, using a bird or ferret as a kind of spy satellite to relay information back to a human "receiving station." But such a skill takes great practice: Animal and human must become very familiar with one another and establish a loving link that lets them translate one another's perceptions. Any one entity usually has a private perceptual spectrum different from any other's, even within a given species. This is partly because sensory input must be translated by the mind, more than by the brain. So when sensory input is second-hand, much less from a different species, a double translation is necessary—with much distortion, unless there has been considerable practice beforehand.

I do not want any misunderstanding as to "lower" or "higher" or "more refined" sensory systems. Every organism develops senses appropriate for its niche in life, and does not improve them pointlessly. In other words, both physical *and* non-physical senses are above all *practical* when initially developed, and only secondarily are expanded or refined for purposes of pleasure. Indeed, a given entity may actually shut down sensory systems that are getting little or no use. This is why cave-dwelling creatures and those in the depths of the seas have abandoned the use of their eyes, even while their sensitivity to vibrations in the electromagnetic spectrum has increased so dramatically as to be difficult for me to describe without several pages' digression.

In such a case, the problems of translation are naturally compounded. A blind cave fish, for example, knows more about electromagnetism than your most accomplished artist knows about color; and the perceptions of the one would be rather difficult to translate into the sensory repertoire of the other.

Yet another variable is intensity. Many organisms have accustomed themselves to responding—or *not* responding—to vastly different levels of stimuli. A desert-dwelling bird is ready for greater glare than, say, a night-hunting owl. Similarly, the volume of sound necessary to communicate with an aging grandparent would be quite too much for a cocker spaniel. And for reasons that are seemingly paradoxical, the subtler the stimulus, the more information it can convey.

Even when direct assumption or assimilation takes place, there is usually an automatic and graceful process of data-digestion on the part of the receiving entity. When mind "speaks" to mind, there is a natural reversion to the lowest of common denominators. For this reason, it is far easier to share emotions with a cat than it is to "see" through that cat's eyes. But even here, a natural accommodation and assimilation are necessary. To the degree to which this does *not* take place, the receiving entity suffers "indigestion."

Such assumption of stray sensory data is actually quite common during the dream state, and often accounts for some of your more unpleasant and bewildering dreams. In such cases, though, the second form of assumption is usually "at fault" and occurs when the receiving entity is out-of-body and more receptive to the emotions, preconceptions, and other *digested* experiences of entities in the vicinity. When out-of-body or in trance, some people will be greedy and gulp down a portion of energy-experience too large to assimilate, much less process effectively. This kind of over-assumption is not dangerous but can be unpleasant, as if a five-year-old nervous system were to take on the energy surge that occurs during an adult orgasm.

In general, overstimulation of the nervous system or psyche is perceived as dis-ease, discomfort, or—at the very extreme—pain. But such does not occur when the mind soaks up emotions, understandings, insights, and other byproducts of consciousness which are *wholly* digested units of experience. These are what you might call the building blocks or molecules of communication, which underlie all languages and systems of syntax. They can be shared effortlessly and with a minimum of translation, since in essence they are *already* translated—basic elements of the universal language. And if put in proper logical order by the arranging mind, they may, when assumed by another entity, give a precise replica of their original cause.

Not only great intellects can leave behind such precise "messages." Indeed, any strong emotion is much like a primary color, ready to be assumed without distortion by another entity of whatever sensitivity. "Proper logical order," then, means simply that the experience was perceived clearly by the original entity and, being held clearly in imaginative memory, can then be later assumed by another entity with only minimal rearrangement. With clear perception, there is less blurring. The digested *result* of sensory or emotional experience is communicated, and not the experience itself.

By contrast, with the first, body/nervous system form of assumption, one is more likely to re-experience the event itself, or sometimes a wild distortion of the original sensory input. You might hear a voice, see a flash of fire, feel a touch upon your hand—but how you then reacted would be up to you. But should you be assuming with your psyche alone, you would hear no voice, but might be heartened by what it had said. You would see no fire, but might feel momentary alarm. You would feel no touch, but might be comforted regardless.

You would, in short, be experiencing the *result*, the *interpretation* of a given experience *as another had interpreted it*. But the more that interpretation diverges from your own, the less practical value that assumption has for you.

In short, I suggest that you perform your own seeing and hearing, emoting and concluding. Do not "assume" that some being of different outlook can do a better job than you can!

Why am I sometimes frightened by the intensity of the energies I receive?

Because you doubt your abilities to handle them. Therefore, when energy comes at you, you have not provided a landing strip for it!

Many of you tune out—or refuse to employ—energies you think would not find a home with you. As a silly example, imagine that you have put off learning how to ski. Yet one night, you have a vivid dream of shushing down the slopes. Waking, you dismiss the dream as fantasy, not recognizing it as an expression of energy that says, "You could do just fine, were you to take to the slopes this weekend."

If you do not give yourselves credit for that which you truly are, you will experience energy as unruly—like a new puppy in the house, too full of beans. But energy *need not* fit into your existence! Energy is less like a puppy than a bloodhound: It will lead you where you need to go, help you find what you have been seeking since you came into this particular incarnation . . . perhaps even before.

So do not worry if energy comes into your house barking and wagging its tail. It will not mess up the rug or chew your slippers, I promise! Unruly energy is only expressing an element of yourself that you have either denied or not used joyously. Rather than repress it, follow it; see where it leads you.

Your Freudians say you repress things you fear. I say, rather, that aspects of your personality get rusty: They become awkward, and you interpret them as evil. A knife, for example, is good for peeling potatoes or sculpting a decoy—yet if it slips and cuts you, it is evil. *It is the tool that is misused, or not used, that your Grander Self is always trying to teach you the use of.* Each of you, without exception, has misused or abandoned some tool that would neatly and gracefully complement your other abilities.

Energy you are learning to experience casts a bright spotlight on your personal tool kit, to show you not only what the tool is, but how best to use it.

I'd like to create powerful, really miraculous changes in my life. Wouldn't such radical changes impinge on other's free will?

If you are going to experience energy, you must open yourself to it *fully.* That is Point Number One. Point Number Two: If you wish to use energy for a miracle, you are free to do so. Point Number Three is the single most important lesson I can leave with you. If you choose—or feel you need—a miracle, it will come tailored to your needs, perfect for your understanding, and ideal for the intent that your Grander Self has chosen for you.

It is virtually impossible for anyone to create someone else's miracle or to *take* someone else's miracle. The flower of a miracle lies in the bud of your being; and it will bloom in your own individualized way. Do not graft another's flower to your own stalk! Beings like me pray that each of you creates your own miracles—for I cannot create the miracles that the lowliest insect in your world can.

You can create miracles of which no one else is remotely capable. And when you create a miracle, it is uniquely your own.

Miracles are not a rare occurrence; they are under your feet, carried within your body even now. By your generous willingness to be receptors and transformers of energies, your world continues to function, your hearts continue to beat, and the very heavens continue to circle over your head.

On the microscopic level, each of you is a tissue of miracles. Yet each of you breathes your own air, pumps your own blood. Each of you is unique, necessarily and vitally so. Even if you block energy, you do it in your own characteristic manner—a learned skill of no mean caliber!

When channeling, I feel accelerated—my heart beats faster, and my energy is expanded. Can you give me feedback on that?

You have kicked up an issue I left hanging before—resonance. In channeling, you make yourself a tuning fork, picking up the thrill a good actor feels when watching a good performance, or an artist feels when going to an art museum. The process works on a telepathic *and* sensory level and is one of the main means of communication throughout your physical universe. Resonance explains how young children can learn so rapidly: Being largely telepathic, they pick up what adults do and how they do it. Resonance is the basis for your "Monkey see, monkey do" and for your parable of the Hundredth Monkey. It is the basis of your learning, your understanding, and your healing, too. Willingness to vibrate with one of a higher capacity is one of the secrets of any form of moving ahead.

To the degree that you shut down and become an individual with your own tastes and preferences, you reduce your ability to resonate with your surrounding colleagues, and your ability to learn *directly* is diminished.

Is resonance, as you describe it, used during dreams?

Yes! In the dream state, you resonate to your own strongest ambitions, as well as to information you have picked up during the preceding *two* days. You are processing the one against the other, which explains why your dreams are frequently so weird.

Why don't people remember more of their dreams?

There are many reasons. Chief among them—most common, I should say—is a belief that "unofficial" dream information is not as reliable as ordinary daytime information.

In a sense, when you go to the land of dreams, you are going to a foreign country where the local currency has pictures of a monarch or a moose on it. When you cross the border again into your waking state, often you go through mental customs and wish to change the "funny money" of the dream state into your more familiar, hard-nosed, practical kind of change.

If you say, "Dreams might be fun to remember, but if I *do* remember them, what good are they?" you are not going to be too highly motivated. The easiest way you can overcome that tendency is by putting your dreams on a higher pedestal: Request that they give you information you *can* use in everyday waking life.

In the dream state, can I communicate with loved ones who have died? If so, would I recall such experiences as vivid dreams?

In such cases, the deceased may be perceived allegorically or—in *your* terms, now—remembered as only "part" of the original whole you may have known in life.

I want to emphasize that the "dead" are not divided up or reduced in any way. Rather, the human unconscious reduces complexities to symbols, to their lowest and most memorable common denominators. Almost all of what you experience in dreams is funneled directly into your unconscious, which must then, when you wake, fling into the shallow bucket of conscious memory as many of its riches as it can. And so, you dismantle your memories of the dead, bringing across the waking threshold only a small fragment of the reality you experienced.

Upon death, your beloved ones quite literally "outgrow" your mind's ability to conceive of and contain them. This inability does not, however, prevent you from continuing—even improving—relationships with individuals you may have enjoyed while they were still "alive," *as long as you are content to pursue these relationships in the dream state.* Again, your misconceptions—or *lack* of conceptions—of the spacious freedom following upon physical death make it hard for you to bring back from your dreams a true, accurate memory of what occurred there.

What is the purpose of Out-of-Body Experiences—particularly if involuntary and not elicited?

Basically, your inner self is playful! There are two different forms of OOBEs, but your researchers have not precise-ified which is which.

The more prominent variety is where the body conscious-ness exercises itself out-of-body. During dreams, it is necessary for the mind to be unplugged so that the body not sleepwalk. The body consciousness does not enjoy having the voluntary nervous system shut down. If it becomes restless, it will project on its own—giving you a very vivid sense of flight, of motion, or of other sensory activity.

The other kind of OOBE is of the mind only. Most of the primary body consciousness is left behind—to watch the store, you might say. In these cases, you do not necessarily remember feelings of bodily motion or projection. You will, however, recall bringing back lessons. You "go off" to be taught, to converse with others whose minds are out of the body.

Those of you who have read Mr. Monroe's *Far Journeys* will remember the two astral bodies of which he speaks. The first "body," which he rises out of, is basically the body consciousness. The projecting "self," you might say, is more purely psyche.

To get back to your question, the mind can play even as the body can. When people tell jokes or play touch football, *parts* of their entire beings are playing. And all OOBEs are, to a degree, play—especially during the night, when many of your everyday rules and regulations are put to bed. Then, various aspects of your psyche can "come out," quite literally!

And all play is basically joyous exploration. Thus, many OOBEs are—in your terms—pointless. You bring back no great information or wisdom, because you have taken the equivalent of a stroll in the woods. But if you return with empty pockets, does that mean you did not get good exercise and fresh air?

What's the most effective method for learning astral projection?

The best way of stimulating *any* journey, to anywhere, is giving yourself a good reason for going there in the first place.

Many of your astral-projection manuals say that after months of arduous discipline, *if* you are successful, you will find yourself bobbing a few inches beneath the ceiling. Big deal!

Rather, if you excite your imagination with the splendors of the Milky Way Galaxy, of ancient Greece or Rome, and make it hungry for possibilities beyond the existence you know, then you can hardly wait to step out of the all-too-familiar. Tempt yourself out of your body the same way you would tempt an animal out of its lair: with a delicious enticement that it can hardly resist.

Very few of you fly aircraft for pleasure. You get on a plane because you have a destination in mind. Give yourself a destination!

Why is it so hard to learn lucid dreaming? It's so important to me, yet it remains so elusive!

Precisely because dreaming *is* important to you, allow it its spontaneity and do not seek to impose lucidity—really, a form of conscious control—upon it.

Those in movie theaters do not keep one eye on the EXIT sign to remind themselves they are watching a movie. Rather, they enter into the arbitrary conventions presented on the screen and "lose" themselves in the story. Much dreaming allows your psyche the same kind of R&R. Lucid dreaming is a contradiction in terms, a means of putting the vagueness and poetry of the dream state under the clear microscope of reason and conscious decisions—which rule the daytime world quite well, thank you!

As you become more playful and spontaneous in your *waking* world, you may expect to "coax" lucid dreams out of hiding, for you will no longer intend to tame them or clip their wings by insisting they play out your waking fantasies. In short, dreams are there to project their images on you, and not the other way around.

Are my recurrent dreams a form of bleed-through from some parallel existence?

Not really! *Recurrent* dreams usually arise from your present life—or more specifically, your present past.

Their stimulus arises from a form of unconscious perfectionism: You may be measuring your worth against not just your own standards, but those of the outside world—and may be unconsciously fighting some value system that has been handed you without your asking. Thus, the dramatizing dream recurs until the conflict is resolved.

Just as a cough tries to eject mucus and sputum, so does the dreaming portion of your unconscious mind seek to eject the value system which you, on a deeper level, recognize as not valid for your current needs. A recurrent dream, then, is a cough of the psyche, a sneeze or hiccup of the unconscious.

In your case, you can stop the "hiccups" by examining the value system you held at the time of the *original* dream in the series, versus your value system *now*. You should see a marked slippage. And once you do, it's easier to understand that the recurrent dream is an exaggeration of what your old value system used to preach.

Dreams must occur in some "place" outside of time. Whenever I experience déjà vu, my reaction isn't, "This is something I've done before," but "This is something I've **dreamed!"**

One of the most frequent functions of dreams is to provide you with opportunities for choices—to preview swatches of experience and samples of events that you may or may not then experience in what you consider to be "real life."

For this reason, dreams often seem surreal: Look in a catalog advertising undergarments, and you will see men and women posed in positions and situations that in real life would appear very strange indeed. Yet as you peruse the catalog, these half-clad, often fragmentary individuals (most of them better looking than the norm) seem right at home, entirely logical. You feel no need to relate to them as people—they are simply models, showing you how a certain product can look *at its best.*

Imagine, then, a catalog of the very worst that can happen —a compendium of loneliness, disaster, and causes for regret. You often thumb through just such mental "catalogs" in your dream states, though the memory of them is often suppressed (as it is, indeed, when you browse through a "good" catalog).

Just as every fashionable garment has its price, so does every positive, happy event demand a certain amount of energy or personal change that you must "pay" in order to undergo the experience. A great many of your root beliefs state that suffering builds character, but this is a distortion. The truth is, many "negative" events lead you through—sometimes via a violent but effective shortcut—to achievements and possibilities that might otherwise have taken you years to attain, if at all. In such cases, you have chosen the most appropriate silver lining, and are merely shopping for your choice of cloud.

Events and experiences you choose *not* to order are, of course, paid far less attention, or not "paid for" at all. Therefore, dream merchandise you do *not* want passes in a confused jumble, similar to what you would see if you riffled through the pages of a catalog. Outdoor boots might be superimposed on a swimsuit; gym equipment on a snowblower. And in the infinite catalog of the dream state, there is all sorts of merchandise to be had. You usually visit several mental "departments" a night to make your advance choices for any single slice of future. Your "budget," in such cases, is virtually unlimited, consisting of the amount of attention or *quantity of consciousness* you are willing to devote to any one situation or event.

You may not buy clothes you can well afford because your closet has no room for them. Similarly, many dream events are not "taken home" because in your waking world, you have not space or time enough to do them justice. You may choose a flat tire on your car simply because such an event comes with "batteries included": It will more or less run its course, like a cold or non-serious illness, leaving most of your consciousness free to concentrate on other details. So in a very real way, a negative event—even an outright disaster—may serve as a psychic time-saver, a way of cutting down on actual "work."

Look on dreams, then, as a delightful shopping experience, where the merchandise is unlimited and the quality every bit as good as you are willing to insist it be. In terms of energy, the very best costs no more than does the shoddy and mediocre.

I want to insert here a few practical pointers on dream shopping. Remember, how something looks in the catalog may be different from how it "fits" when it finally is delivered. If you are not satisfied with any reality, it is usually within your power to send it back and request a replacement. Also, if you wake from a troublesome and frightening dream, it is wise to "cancel the order." Tell yourself that, having experienced that given event in the dream state, you have no need or desire for an instant replay in physical reality.

Lastly, remember that many dream items are back-ordered or must be shipped in bulk lots. For example, a beautiful child may not arrive until you have a truly loving spouse and a safe household in which to raise her. Do not ask for a rare goldfish before settling on water, and a tank. Most events bear with them a number of necessary accessories, and often, your reluctance to accept these extras—"Oh, that is not what I ordered!"—delays or even cancels the order for what you most deeply desire.

Let's say I have a clear vision that seems precognitive. How can I tell if that event is going to manifest in this reality?

If you perceive a large shiny purple grapefruit in the air in front of you, grab it and try to slice it. If you can make purple grapefruit juice, you cannot class it as a vision!

As is the case with dreams, visions—even symbolic ones—serve as a form of catalog. You can say, "I will accept this given vision, but let it be brown or red, not purple!" Visions are an imaginative way of letting you experience things beyond your normal sensory range, just as a catalog is.

Can we send a reality back, then?

You can indeed! Say, "I do not want this reality. I wish it to pass away from me." Or you can say, "This is the wrong size, the wrong color. I wish it to come in a different form that fits me better." Or—and this is a mantra you should be able to use without hurting anybody's feelings—say, "It does me no *good* to wear a reality that does not fit me."

By accepting a reality that does not fit you, you are in a sense depriving a probable someone else who *does* need that reality for a perfect fit.

Then are some visions of other probable realities?

Precisely, even as a catalog is a bleed-through of merchandise that you cannot directly perceive, but may be on sale several hundred miles away.

If a vision recurs several times, can I test it to see whether it's from a probable reality?

Simply place it in whatever reality you choose! Tomorrow morning is a reality that you cannot now perceive with your normal five senses, yet you will agree that tomorrow morning "exists." What if a vision shows up again and again? In a catalog, you may find many images of a given product—say, a VCR. Seemingly, the VCRs will be there to haunt you. You may think, "How may I exorcise these images of VCRs?"

If you have a specific image that recurs, you are very efficiently precise-ifying your desires—which each of you, in your own way, is trying to do. Seeing an image in various replicas of itself, you can whittle down to where your true interest lies. You are teaching yourself effectively, efficiently—above all, *safely*—to become expert in discriminating the quality of these recurring images.

Then should I trust that things will eventually wind up the way they're supposed to?

Yes, even if they do not manifest themselves in physical reality at all!

This is an important point that none of you should ever forget: Having experienced something in imagination, in a vision, in a dream takes you off the hook to a degree. Simply by experiencing it in thought, you have in a sense paid your learner's fee or trial subscription. Unless further acquaintance with this event will be truly nourishing to your psyche, chances are you might as well pass it up.

This should not be any great surprise: It explains why many perceived visions and realities do not come to pass—or happen in a seemingly distorted or altered way.

If we finally get to the bottom of all of our belief systems, then what happens?

Here comes the basic lesson: Your beliefs—assumptions, prejudices, wishful thinkings, and daydreams—are requests and invitations. Though this may seem harsh, your fears and anxieties are *also* invitations.

As the "host," you are responsible for whatever realities you choose to invite through your beliefs. Do not forget to choose, or else your old beliefs out of the past will do your choosing for you.

I have trouble—have had trouble—conceiving of how time can be simultaneous. And I will have trouble unless you can help me out!

If there were a statue in the middle of this room, each of you could perambulate about the statue, looking at it from different sides. You would agree that its outline changed as you moved around it, but at no time would you assume that the statue itself was changing. Were it of a general on horseback, no matter whether you were looking at the end holding the sword or the end with the horse's tail, you would recognize that it was a single statue.

Now, during our afternoon here, you perceive what you think of as a sequence of instants. In reality—in *my* terms—this entire afternoon exists as one substance, you might say, even though it may be perceived in different ways as you move through it.

Your perception of time is a means of looking at a Whole Event from all of its "sides." Therefore, if you ask me to predict the future, your "future" in *my* terms may be the other side of the statue which you cannot yet see. However, free will is operative, so that if you arrive at the other end of the statue and are gazing in a different direction, you may not experience what I thought you would. I cannot accurately predict how the statue will appear to you if I do not know at what "time" you will arrive to view it.

We are talking about *real* time in *my* terms, and illusionary time in three-dimensional terms. The sculptor sculpts his statue in *real* time, knowing how it will be perceived—but in illusionary time, the spectators must walk all the way around it, in order to grasp what the sculptor intended.

To put it another way, the entire symphony exists upon your compact disk, but you must let your laser beam go 'round and 'round to unwind the music, you might say. In what you *think* is linear time, you unroll events to examine them, even as you unroll your tape recordings. From my point of view, events are all rolled up into one, exactly like one big ball of yarn—and visible that way.

Although I cannot accurately predict when you will be at a given place, I can say, "This is your *conditional* future: If you do not touch your CD player, you will be at the Fifth Movement in 22 minutes." But of course, if you wish to change your disk or to replay something, that is up to you. My prediction hinges on there being no changes.

But very few of you move in straight lines, without alteration. You make many turns, for many of the same reasons as you do when you drive a car. Steering in one direction only, you would swiftly go into the ditch. You make changes according to the lay of the land, according to too many variables to predict—unless you have agreed to meet under the clock at the Biltmore at such-and-such an hour. If I can predict *that*, it is because *you* have chosen to be there, not because I have used any "occult" powers.

PART THREE

Where

You

Are

Headed

7

Desire and Destiny

• Dynamics of romantic attraction • Sex and—not versus—spirituality • Eros and agape • The proper goals of a relationship • The psychology of single parents • Promiscuity, masochism, and sexual obsession • A new definition of monogamy • Wishes versus intents: how everyday impulses affect your overall evolution

What are the sexual dynamics of the attraction of younger men to women old enough to be their mothers—and vice versa?

Are you ready for a rather lengthy lecture on sex? Good—and if you can please cease your wild cheering, I will begin.

At the heart of *any* sexual relationship is a basic paradox: You will always find yourself in "love" with, or attracted to, *both* a specific individual and a general archetype. And that, ideally, should force you to think about larger issues than simple sexuality *per se.*

It would not be inaccurate to compare the physical aspects of the human race to a vast garden, in which flowers of every imaginable proportion, color, size, and shape flourish, interbreed, and pass away. It is very difficult for any one individual to embrace the whole of mankind, and so, as individuals, you specialize. When someone says, "You are not my type," he or she is not denying you membership to the human race, only stating that as a would-be beloved, you do not fit the criteria for mating that this individual has set up. Just as one man may grow roses and not orchids, gloxinias and not marigolds, so some individuals will, within any particular life, specialize in the kind of mate they choose. You might say they prefer to enter the Garden of Humanity through a deliberately narrow door. In your past, some gardens were constructed with cunning entrances to narrow the visual focus of whomever entered in, to artificially direct attention to specific points of interest—in short, to emphasize what the fashion of the age considered important.

Now, those who thus restrict their sexual ambitions have an interest that is primarily aesthetic. They are most interested in *quality*—which need not be of great duration. "Youth and beauty are fleeting," such people affirm, "and so, we may as well fuck them on the fly, as it were." Just as a skier shushes through virgin snow he knows will melt a few months hence, being intent on a "good run" and not on whatever long-term benefits the crisp winter air and exercise will bring him, so the sexual aesthete plows through as many snowy virgins as possible. The goal—consciously held, now—is "the good life," living in such a way that one may treasure the memories forever and effortlessly command the envy of others.

To return to our garden analogy, some horticulturists are not so interested in having the biggest gladiolus on the block, as in the entire nurturing *process* of gardening. They take joy in the simple warmth of sun on the back of their hands. They do not begrudge the sore backs they get from weeding. They take pleasure from composting and irrigation, from watching the soil bring forth a seemingly chaotic and unplanned array of flowers and vegetables, trees and vines. Such people can even take pleasure in weeds, and will cultivate with great love some poor, scraggly wastrel rescued from the roadside.

And because they take pleasure in the pure delight of green leaves, in the *overall* patterns of change and development in the vegetable kingdom, their garden is perhaps not so crowded with prizewinners and peak experiences. The pleasure they harvest is slower, more steady—and more pervasive.

Now, as far as sexuality is concerned, this second kind of person will not be as attracted by a ripe breast or corn-tassel shock of blond hair as by character—by personality, not so much as looks. They will fall in "love" with anyone who best distills humanity's finest qualities: health, generosity, humor, ability of the non-showing-off kind, and wisdom. Such people may seem perverse or unconventional, plucking from the Garden of Humanity the most unlikely nosegays, and

potting up to take home weird species and contorted speci-
mens that no sexual aesthete would bother with. But then,
their pleasure comes from the process, not from dazzling
instants of perfection and culmination.

Thus on the one hand, you have the perennial romantics,
the playboys, the good-time-Charlies, the promiscuous Don
Juans, people of either gender who spend effort in the gym
and time at the hair stylist. On the other hand, you have the
mothers, the long-term lovers, the friends who drift in and out
of bed with each other and still maintain their friendship—and
yes, the older women and younger men. Again, this second
group is more interested in humanity's deeper health, and so
will enter the Garden by whatever entrance seems appropriate
—by whatever door is closest to a healthy, robust example of
what is best about human life.

I hasten to add that neither type is pure. Many of you will
combine in yourselves more than a little of both types. You may
be attracted to an unconventional partner simply because that
individual is a rather prime specimen in terms of looks, or
in terms of pleasuring ability. But when attraction cuts across
the normal limitations, it is not usually for so fleeting a goal.
Usually, now, the unconventional romance is fed by deeper qualities and ambitions than can be commonly discovered on your
Best Dressed List.

Many unconventional romances are begun simply because
they are, on the face of it, unlikely. Therefore, the participants
have the added kick of defying convention. (Because very few
of you make love 24 hours a day, *any* romance or affair brings
with it the slight whiff of unconventionality, of something
above and beyond the norm.) They may enjoy the extra effort
it takes to keep the relationship alive—for the same reasons
some parents rejoice in encouraging a young child's independence, and others take pride in nursing the runt of the litter to
full health.

Still others will take on an unconventional romance as a
means of avoiding blame: "How could you expect it to last?
I was old enough to be his mother!" But usually, such unconventional lovers are bedazzled by what they know to be
good, true—and eternal—in Man and not dependent on age,
looks, or whatever type is In this season. And so, they tunnel

through the walls of the Garden in their own way, making a beeline for the specimen that most promises to nourish their ever-evolving wisdom.

Now, do not for a moment think that I am letting you same-age, different-gender couples off the hook. You may be exactly as unconventional as a 90-year-old black woman living with a 16-year-old Norwegian track star. Indeed, your temperaments and goals in life may well be at great variance and cross-purposes. But in a way, the more *similar* you are, the greater is your challenge. It is easier to make allowances for anyone raised in another culture, another language, another generation—but if someone has had the same advantages and education and breeding as you, what is his or her excuse? Thus, many "perfect" couples break up, while many unconventional ones stay together by working out a system of mutual tolerance and by welcoming each other's differences.

One who begins as a sexual aesthete may finish as one in love with humanity in general—a common and praiseworthy course. But that is not to disparage the white-haired gent who takes a hankering to a granddaughter's friend, on the basis of looks alone. There are no rules in love, but these three:

Thou shalt not violate thy beloved's integrity,

And thou shalt not violate what thou knowest to be thine own highest purpose—

Nor *allow* it to be violated out of so-called love for another!

Ideally, love of whatever sort is both an incentive and an opportunity for learning. When it ceases to be so, much of the flavor is gone. The main trick is to seek emotional nourishment and not just the spice of life, to love with your heart even as you do with your eyes. And to do so, you must avoid allegorizing excessively—you must sense the humanity and indwelling god-spark in the other even as you cherish him or her as a unique individual.

Romance, you see, *always* sees its goal as singular; whereas agape, the love-of-mankind, *always* sees its goal as plural, as universal. These are the main axes of romantic alignment, and where they meet is yet another crossroads that any couple must traverse. But it is quite easy to shift from one axis to another —which is why many relationships take apparent right-angle turns and transmute themselves utterly, not once but several times.

The "purely" sexual axis also displays a similar polarity: At the one extreme of the axis is the sex-as-leisure enthusiast, and at the other, the only-for-propagation proponent. It would mortify them both to know that each is right! And it may startle you to realize that the more layers of competing opposites you can fold into a relationship, the stronger it will become, much as a Japanese sword is doubled and folded, doubled and folded by the smith before finally being annealed into an instrument of matchless integrity.

And so, I ask you to be *more* sexy, not less—but also, to stop restricting your definitions of what sex must, can, and should be. For in the morning of the millennium, the Garden of Mankind will have its walls thrown down. And you who already know the paths, eschewing the doors of convention, will never have to worry about losing your way.

I wish to add that for too many of you, *love* is a somewhat manipulative verb. It has hooks, and presupposes a certain standard of behavior upon those on whom it is not-always-so-generously offered. Instead, I say that I *approve and appreciate* you fully— and bid you approve and appreciate one another, even as I do you.

Over the centuries, some on a spiritual path have chosen to sublimate their sexual energies. Could you address that dynamic?

I can indeed, because in your question are several places where logic is strained and the fit is not exact.

Too often your religious leaders, East and West, have taught that the body has only so much energy. Therefore, if you wish to obtain spirituality *and* your sexual engines are running full blast, you may not have the gas to make it up Parnassus. The corollary of that has been, "If you wish to grow apples badly enough, you can squeeze and mortify orange trees until they finally come up with apples."

I am here to tell you that there are apples *and* oranges. Yes, there is sex; yes, there is spirituality. I'm not saying, "Never the twain shall meet." Nor are they at automatic loggerheads; nor does the practice of one necessarily inhibit achievement—scoring, if you will—in the other. Would a spiritually *in*volved and *e*volved being not use his or her sexuality in a spiritual way? Why would there be any contradiction?

Often, what you think of as "blatant sexuality" is nonspiritual manifestations of that very energy. Therefore, they *are* the more blatant. Your culture has not learned how to express sexuality automatically, in a spiritual way. Many of *you* have discovered how, but because you are doing it on a spiritual level, you do not brag or compare notes. In your culture, therefore, it seems unknown.

I am not a peeping Thomas, but I can tell you that spiritual sexuality is at the heart of every true loving relationship. And in its further reaches, sexuality encompasses more of the etheric body than of the physical body. Much of what you think of as love at first sight is not the result of physical instincts or hormones but rather, the intertwinings of the energy body.

Some of you have read it is possible to make love on the astral plane; so it is. There are only so many ways boy can meet girl; but an enormous number of ways in which two individuals' energy bodies can interreact. And your energy body extends approximately 150 feet in all directions! If, conceptually or anatomically, you restrict sexuality to your sexual organs, you are shortchanging not only yourself, but whomever you have chosen as your partner. If your intent is to be spiritual, your sexuality will automatically follow suit, automatically helping you along your path.

People using their guruhood to seduce comely disciples are not dealing honestly. As long as *you* deal honestly with your fellow human beings, both your spirituality and your sexuality are more likely to be successful. I don't think I'll have any disagreement on either count.

I'm attracted only to specific types of men. Am I missing something by being so discriminating? Entities always tell us to love unconditionally—but does that include romantic love as well?

You all, male or female, are movie projectors. To a greater or lesser degree, your "beloveds" are screens.

When you are young, you tend to prefer the whitewashed, untouched screen. That is why so many of your 19th-century roués preferred virgins: They desired a screen on which to present their fantasies without any alteration whatever. All of you, however, share the same conundrum: To what degree do you wish to project yourself upon a screen that has held previous images?

Of course, such previous images—even if visible—are healthy for you, because your "film" need never change in response. Whether you project it upon a good screen or a worn and dirty surface, you can always run it again elsewhere. Your film, in those terms, is what you want to perceive, what you want to find visible, in others. Using that analogy, all of you are film students—studying how your hopes and desires are projected upon external reality. If you are alive, you are also learning.

Each of you knows someone upon whom you have projected your personal desires, and who did not distort them. Perhaps you were in love with that person *because* he or she reproduced your thoughts and desires so faithfully—the Pygmalion myth addresses both artists and romantics! Yet there are others you detest, who seem to have transmuted and distorted your finest ideals completely. In fact, your ideals have *not* been altered, but the distorter helps you see them in a new and enlightening way.

You, as a physical being, are a lens. What you perceive as your highest goal is the "show" you project outward. Physical reality—"out there," as you think of it—is your screen. *But the lens can distort what it receives back, even though what reaches the screen may be in perfect focus!* And once you understand that others are projecting *their* own movies upon parts of the same screen, then you begin to see the difficulty —and yes, the delight!—of the dilemma you presented to yourself by incarnating in the first place.

I am trying *not* to wean you away from your normal thought patterns. Rather, I am asking you to take a different look at your reality-screens. Recognize that, just as you can delight in watching clouds form or fish swim, enjoying what lies beneath or above you, so you can explore and appreciate another human's reality even if you never "possess" or inhabit it.

Once you understand *that*, you will have the key to all questions of love that you could ever ask me, or yourselves. Once you understand that you can be part of one thing and yet fully appreciate something else, then you understand love. You do not need to possess, either in physical reality or in terms of time. As long as you can approve and appreciate, you are the winner of *that* game of marbles. Even if someone else takes home the physical marbles, yet you take home the essence of the game, the beauty of the individual marbles—and of the individual you played with.

Now, when I say you play games, I am not putting you down at all. I play games on *my* level, and you revere some who play football and basketball on your level. Yet you know perfectly well that master chess champions, with the clocks ticking and the cameras rolling, are not enjoying their match—so why should you be under the gun when you love?

In chess, of course, your opponents teach you how to play. I say it is both your lovers and your worst enemies—whom you think of as your opponents—who teach you how to play. If you are lucky, you will find a good opponent whom you love, and he will teach you how to play. Should you not find such a man, you will again and again find individuals who challenge your game.

You are potential champions, each of you. Not for strategy's or for winning's sake, but for enjoyment's sake, learn how to play the game! You all knew how to lose and laugh, but you forgot. And when you remember—or learn anew—to lose and giggle, all the pieces of opportunity will be put back on the board, and you may pursue a new game—or a new opponent.

Why are some gay men so very promiscuous?

It is important to distinguish between the *choice* of being gay, which we have discussed already, and the mechanisms by which that choice is effected.

Too frequently, an individual is highly motivated sexually because he or she feels deficient in a given trait. Your nymphomaniac, for example, is said to crave attention, and seeks it by using her sexual behavior as a lure. In many instances, the promiscuous individual of either sex, of whatever sexual preference, seeks to prove something to him- or herself—to seek in a series of other individuals that which is felt to be personally lacking.

I am in no way condemning or criticizing those who are attracted to their own sex, but only warn that if they seek others out of a lack of self-worth, they are bound to be disappointed. They are broadcasting into the world a mixed signal, to wit:

"I do not believe myself attractive—or masculine, or dashing, or witty—but I will pretend to be so by seeking out a partner with those same qualities. But since I do not share in these qualities, the other I seek is bound to leave me, once he or she discovers my 'low bank account,' as it were."

This attempt to deceive the self by deceiving others results in a great deal of what you call obnoxious sexual behavior, as well as rapes and other crimes of sexual violence. Attempts to sleep with either gender, *when one is merely treating the other as an allegorical or symbolic figure and not as a human being*, are of course doomed to end badly. For the inner self is not fooled for long, any more than chronic pain can be dispelled by a series of aspirins.

Pain, of whatever sort, is a signal that a healing change is called for. And to assume that a compensatory loved one will cure your poor self-image is tantamount to assuming that a shot of Novocaine will cure your toothache.

I'd like to ask about sadomasochism, as practiced by consenting adults. Is it healthy?

How healthy it is depends largely on how it originates.

Your masochists are, in a sense, healthier than the sadists, because they have less need to control their sexual partners. They are more trusting than the sadist, who is usually deeply afraid of his or her own sexual identity and believes that no other individual will "hold still" for him or her unless bound and gagged. In other words, the infliction of pain or restraint upon another during sex—even by way of play-acting—is a more or less tacit admission that you do not trust partners to come your way on their own and, on a most basic level, expect them to be indifferent or to reject you outright.

The masochist, as your psychologists have pointed out, usually equates sex with evil of one sort or another, but guilt about sex is not the motive. Guilt seldom seeks out its own punishment; or at least tends to do so at some remove—either through remorse on the morning after, or by coming down with some physical affliction that may or may not be a sexually transmitted disease. Those ridden with guilt over sex, then, want to have their cake and eat it too—but not at the same time.

The masochist, rather, usually associates sex with unpleasant, aggressive behavior on the part of another. Perhaps a punitive/seductive adult or parent of either sex prompted the young mind to equate cruelty with charm and attractiveness. It is not necessary for incest or abuse to occur for such an equation to be made. Now, masochists seek to *control* whatever dangers they perceive by placing the violence they associate with sex in a ritualized, and therefore confined, context. There, what is deeply perceived as dangerous can be experienced safely.

Zoo visitors often delight in getting close to the bars of the tiger's cage or in pressing their noses against the glass of the cobra's den. The masochist has much the same impulse: to experience the dangerous within the context of safe and reassuring barriers. How much healthier if these zoo visitors could see the tiger and the cobra as their colleagues upon Earth, and not feel the need to distance themselves with bars or shatterproof glass!

Animals of whatever species react quite naturally to one's unspoken fears. And it would be far healthier if individuals did not approach each other in leather armor, as if ready to do battle, but met as colleagues who could be trusted without benefit of ritual, contract, or previously agreed-upon script.

If someone is obsessed with me—or his image of me—does that give him any actual power or advantage?

It all depends on what *aspect* of the obsessee the obsessor chooses to attach. That is, most individuals tend to allegorize one another, focusing on one or two attributes and defects to the exclusion of all else.

If you are proud or ashamed of some facet of your being, and should another's value judgments happen to agree with yours, your own beliefs will be pushed—or accelerated—thereby, simply because they are in such close harmony. But if another wishes you good health while you yourself want to be safe in the hospital and out of harm's way—if the other's desire and yours are *not* mutual—then the effect will be minimal, if at all.

If obsession had any intrinsic power, then beautiful women and handsome men would almost always be promiscuous and yet virtuous in most other ways, simply by obeying others' stereotypes of how the good-looking behave.

If enough energy is directed in one person's direction, the sheer amount of that energy *can* cause side effects—but will be expressed, say, in a stumble or in an accession of strange ideas, perhaps "inappropriate" exhilarations and enthusiasms. Because those thoughts are not properly "coded," they will not affect their object's intent or desires. Just as the pollen of a dahlia will not fertilize an oak, so are "foreign-of-purpose" thoughts ignored by the receiving entity.

This is also why love can be so ecstatic: Laser light at long last, after years of muddled glows!

If one party is non-physical, will the obsession have greater or lesser force?

Simply because non-physical entities are more easily swayed by thought, they will be more easily attracted to a physical entity "beaming out" given thought patterns related to them. But they can choose not to come when called! Holding a non-physical entity's name or likeness in mind gives you no power over that entity.

It *can* be that an incarnate may find him- or herself "moody" if a non-physical entity is brooding about that incarnate's welfare. But anyone possessing a body can radiate or at least *amplify* more energy. In this regard, the corporeal one has the advantage.

Also, obsessions tend to have more strength—and to last longer—on the physical plane, simply because gratification there is so often delayed. If you can quickly create and run through any number of delightful possibilities, as I can, said possibilities swiftly pale unless they have great appeal indeed.

In short, obsessions usually represent blocked thinking: an inability to get around or through given obstacles inherent in physical reality. The obsessive personality is not versatile and is thus more likely to be an incarnate, to whom the possibilities of versatility are more carefully hidden.

Why can a physical *entity amplify more energy? I thought it would be the other way around.*

Simply, a physical entity has a body—which, in the physical world, acts as a rather powerful creator and amplifier of energies. You cannot amplify energies in *my* reality any more efficiently than I can in yours—that is, I can manipulate energies in your reality, but not nearly as easily or effectively as I can in my own.

Similarly, there is little you can do to swerve the course of the planets above your head. But within your own reality— your own chosen arena of action—there is very little your energies *cannot* accomplish, few energies you cannot directly manipulate.

It is up to you, of course, to define your personal sphere of action and determine, in your own mind, where it should justly stop. You should not—and need not—influence realities and entities about which you are utterly indifferent.

There is a connection, then, between an obsessor and an obsessee—but it only goes in one direction. If you are moon-struck, the moon is in no way responsible for your plight. Similarly, should a stranger fall in love with you on sight, you need not give permission for such an event to occur. Only if you choose to *react* to that individual are patterns of any kind established in the other direction—and even so, they are very weak. In most such cases, you will simply ignore individuals who do not interest you, to the point of not even noticing their attentions.

No obsession has very great transferable power, you see, because the obsessor invariably focuses on a rather *minor* attribute of the obsessee—on a rather minor lump of the toad, you might say. Extending that analogy will explain a number of your fetishes.

In nature, of course, there are signs, scents, signals, court-ing behaviors—but these are sort of smoke signals intended to bring together interested parties, who may then go on to larger goals that are not necessarily sexual. Imagine a shipwrecked sailor who sends up a flare. A rescue plane approaches, nets the flare out of midair, and returns whence it came. It is similarly sad when an obsessive one mistakes the flare for the individual who launched it, for the flare, spectacular though it may be, is hardly as durable or as marvelous as the one who sent it aloft.

All of us—and all of *you*, I should add—are continually sending up flares. Those who do so compulsively, out of a sheer love of fireworks, are known as flirts. That can be a bright and happy sport, unless it becomes manipulative: "Let's see how many rescue planes I can get to lift off *this* time!" When another reads more into your communication or performance than you intended, it is your responsibility to limit your meaning, and instruct that person out of his or her ignorance. Flares come in all intensities and colors, and the dim flare of misunderstanding is the one that you most consistently ignore.

My partner and I always want different things out of life. As a result, our relationship isn't so hot. Any advice?

The relationship as a whole needs a goal. If you are making the mistake of saying, "This relationship is cramping my style," or "He always wants me to be different," then you are viewing one another as individuals who must fit together *perfectly*.

Each of you should be a component in the relationship, but still separate enough to do his or her thing. The relationship should enable you to do your thing better—both as individuals *and* jointly. If you do not accomplish anything better together than you could separately—or with anyone else—then the relationship will die.

What does the *relationship* want to achieve and accomplish? It must provide you a higher freedom in which to work; it must have a goal that would be impossible for either of you to meet as individuals.

I'm married, but reluctant to have children. Plus I'm thinking a lot about my old boyfriend, who's having trouble launching his musical career. I'd like to get back in touch with him. Which relationship is right for me?

As you will understand, no single relationship is "right" for you. The better question is, which relationship is right for your purpose or overall intent?

My impression is that you have used your current marriage as a sort of ledge, or resting place, during which time you have replenished the resources remaining in your grip and planned to try a second assault on the peak of your desires—from which peak or pinnacle you had previously found yourself repulsed.

In either case, win or fail, you will be breathing rarefied air and be closer to your goals; but at present, you find yourself dissatisfied at not having made a more daring attempt. It may reassure you that several years ago, you would not have been able to employ many of the skills that you now enjoy in communicating with a loved one. Developing these abilities was, of course, one of the larger purposes of your marital "time out."

You can indeed be happy if you remain with your current husband, as long as you recognize that another individual cannot define or create happiness for you, except as that individual enables you to fulfill your chosen goals. To put that backwards: As long as what you need to be happy is not currently being *withheld* by that individual—why, no problem!

Your decision regarding children has been akin to a mountain climber saying, "Let me not peg my tent down too tightly, lest I be forced to camp here forever and lose the opportunity to climb higher." May I recall to you that children *per se* are not a goal; raising them most certainly is. And thus, it is best to choose the proper father or "raiser"—who will allow you to set your own instinctive best goals for those children. Children will come of themselves when you are emotionally ready to receive them and can see no possibility that they will constrain you from wider achievements in addition to child rearing.

Now, your musician friend is somewhat conflicted as to whether his gift needs be used for profit and outward recognition, or should be nurtured as a private thing to delight the near and dear as well as himself. Your own view of career-versus-talent rather complements his. So, with your assistance and feedback, this musician can decide which is the hub of the musical experience, and which the perimeter—for him. Is playing in public the fast-moving rim that "gets him rolling"? Or does he prefer to focus his attention on the inner power of the music—the axle, you might say—and let his career-wheel be steered where it will?

There are tires and there are driveshafts, and the only tragedy is if one cannot decide which one wishes to be.

If a woman really wants to raise a family, why would she keep choosing love affairs that she knows will be temporary?

Many of your women are choosing to be single parents— either having the baby without getting married, or else divorcing the husband soon after the baby is born. This is the flip side of the situation embodied and described in the previous answer. In either case, the woman trusts children as extensions of herself —but does *not* trust men, who must be taken "as is," warts and all. She can mold and raise a child as she sees fit. Men, however, are already raised and molded and thus present a threat.

Therefore, the woman who keeps running across "wrong" partners may be seeking a family to *raise*, rather than a family to *be a part of.* The give-and-take inherent in any long-term relationship does not appeal to her, and so she will select fragile relationships that are easily broken out of, whether or not these result in pregnancy. A woman who chooses "wrong" partners may also be seeking to demonstrate the superiority of herself or her gender as a whole. To be fair, I would suggest that many men run on a similar program, continually seeking out "problem" relationships so that the damning evidence will be crystal clear to any third party and that they may be exonerated from any blame for those relationships' failure.

Martyrs come in both sexes, and often try to prove their martyrhood by having children.

Could you give us your definition of monogamy?

I'd be surprised if we could leave this topic so quickly! Monogamy, as I define it for you, is the art of doing one thing at a time, with one partner. You need not be with the same person till death do you part. However, no matter who you are with, I recommend you give to that relationship all you feel it demands of you—give it a break, you might say.

A relationship, as many of you are aware, has a life of its own, as if by coming together, the two of you produced a third entity that can surprise you both. It may have "inherited" your good as well as your bad points. *A* may find himself getting a bit nasty, yet *B* has her best brought out. Why is this? Because in their own sneaky way, sexuality and love relationships are meant to focus you back on your life's purpose, on areas where you are imbalanced. When you find difficulty or inadequacy in yourself, these private shortcomings will project themselves outward and "incarnate"—not necessarily in offspring or in your partner, but in the relationship itself.

If you look upon the *relationship* as what you must be true to, that will help you understand the function and proper practice of monogamy. Yes, you can cheat on a person without him or her knowing and get away scot-free. You cannot do so with the relationship, however, for if you are not "true" to it, you automatically withdraw energy from it, and it suffers accordingly. Now, there are forms of energy that will not take effect right away, so the good effort you put into a relationship may unexpectedly flower—come to its strength and conclusion—only several months or years afterwards.

I do not want you to think that by negative thinking, you can poison a relationship and have it go sour years later. The mind regularly rids itself of poisonous and inappropriate thought material, often through anger. This is why it is healthy to express your emotions and release whatever is bothering you, and why it is disagreeable for others to be around while you do so—as if you invited loved ones into the room while you defecated or vomited!

So, all of you must constantly make this decision, this trade-off: "To what degree am I going to use my relationship as a receptacle for what I have to bring out of myself? How can I express myself without polluting the relationship unto death?" That is a *question* I offer you. I cannot give you the answer, for some relationships exist *only* so that they may serve as receptacles. For a relationship to grow, however, it must function on other levels as well. There are no rules, no way it *must* be. It is up to you, jointly and individually, to determine what you want in a relationship.

Many of you think a relationship is like a sports car, a house in the country, or a trip to Puerto Rico—something consummately desirable, what everyone would want. Yet if you give three different people the same automobile, each of them will drive it to a different destination. Send those same three people to Puerto Rico, and each will amuse him or herself in a different way. When someone says, "relationship," do not assume that he or she is thinking of the relationship *you* have in mind.

This will sound like a paradox: Even though two strangers have a one-night stand, they can nevertheless have a most valid relationship! Duration is not the only way in which a relationship can succeed. Even if the relationship dies, even though it lasts for three hours, the two partners may see themselves—and each other—more clearly. It might be, for example, that our two strangers can, by their approval and appreciation of one another, express their *generalized* love —and yes, sexual attraction—for all of humanity. They may use each other, exploit each other, but so joyously and approvingly—and yes, spiritually—that each comes away fulfilled and augmented from their encounter.

By using this specific example, you can see how, if lovers choose to fantasize, imagining their partner as Tom Selleck or Raquel Welch, they are not being faithful to their *relationship*.

So many of my friends changed after they got married. Ever since I got engaged, I've been worrying about marriage being so final, really locking me in.

That problem arises only if you perceive marriage as a goal, as the culmination of the attraction process. Each of you should perceive your marriage as a *tool* with which you can accomplish more efficiently the task you have already begun. To the extent that your idea of marriage represents something fixed—a diminution of your abilities and freedoms—then certain opportunities are being put to bed against their will. They may wake up later, at inopportune times, to cause you much unrest and anxiety.

Marriage, then, should represent a new area that gives you two *more* space, not less, to continue your alchemical improvements of one another. Not that you need wholly redefine your concept of marriage, but you should agree, discuss, and investigate *together* what you are *already* doing jointly and how marriage will affect and improve your "efficiency."

In other words, view marriage as an accessory to the relationship you already enjoy. That relationship, after all, is the soul of whatever marriage takes place. Therefore, the marriage should be worthy of the relationship, and not the other way around.

Try to make your transition into marriage—should you choose to make it—as natural and graceful as it should ideally be. I do not want either of you standing on an imaginary cliff, bracing for a broad-jump, wondering what will happen if you do not "make it across" to the very end of your days. Rather, I prefer that you wake one day to find yourself married, as you might wake to discover that spring had come, and that it was now warm enough to make those improvements that the rainy winter had prevented.

If unfulfilled wishes can awaken later "at inopportune times," then are we hampered by hopes and desires we had long ago, even as far back as childhood—sort of like psychological land mines that make it difficult and dangerous to move freely?

You have to distinguish between a *wish* and the underlying *intent*. For example, on a very hot day, you might wish to be immersed in a cool mountain stream. But this would represent only a whim of the moment, dictated by temporary circumstances, and would hardly reflect your life's purpose. You would not want to live out your old age permanently under water.

So it is with unfulfilled wishes. For the most part, they *are* fulfilled in some other system of probabilities and are thus "defused" or deactivated. Using your land-mine analogy, they are allowed to expend their energy harmlessly on a safe testing range. But they can also leave behind them what I might call fossil desires. That is, a particularly poignant or deeply felt whim can so impress its outline on the subconscious memory that a *replica* of that desire can, as I said, later come awake. It is a cast of the original desire, and not the original—

though being of the same size and proportions, it will function exactly as the original did, for all intents and purposes.

Desires, like the personalities that create them, evolve. It is in their nature to do so. Just as a growing tree constantly swaddles its twigs in fresh new wood, so does any desire, however small, eventually expand and broaden, or else merge with others—so that, like the slowly widening limb of a tree, it may transmit more and more of the experience of life. To a degree, temporary whims and wishes are under the "gravitational pull" of the parent entity's overall life-intent or larger purpose. If, for example, you are enamored of spiritual knowledge above all else, your desires for wine, women, and song might be refracted into a desire for holy communion, for the writings of St. Teresa, and for hymns and sacred music.

Freud would have called this sublimation, but it is rather a process of attraction. A tree's branches are shaped by—and often grow perpendicularly to and in apparent "defiance" of—gravity; so are any entity's desires shaped (or in a very few cases, distorted) by that entity's larger intents, *at least as far as the acting-out or fulfillment of those desires is concerned.*

A nuclear scientist and a Trappist monk may both experience the exact same urge for an ice-cream cone. Yet how these men answer their desires will depend on their larger overall purpose. The scientist may use the ice cream as an excuse to treat his children and return, however briefly, to a world of flesh and blood; while the monk may deny himself the pleasure and instead offer up his desire as a sacrifice to God. Yet their initial craving—even down to the specific flavor of the ice cream—may have been identical.

Why do you devote so much attention to questions about sexual obsession?

Simply because any obsession or isolated craving represents a serious departure from normal growth in the psyche. In the body, you have serious conditions arising when organs or systems fail to mature normally; so are there health-threatening implications to the psyche when a given desire does not develop properly.

Healthy love quickly learns to generalize: The sight of the beloved's face (stimulus of the original attraction) soon expands into a non-sexual affection for that person's speech, habits, and ways of thinking. But a love that is too specific is actually quite akin to hatred! Just as repugnance or anger is a means of isolating things that need removal from one's immediate surroundings, so can a too-finicky and too-particular love isolate its cherished goal from the entire fabric of the lover's daily life.

You have all heard of collectors who keep their goodies locked up, away from the light of day. Just so, many sexual obsessions become increasingly private and thus, are not able to expand and generalize as they should. The attraction to *any* specific is merely a means, a goad, to entice you to learn more, understand and appreciate more, of what is out there around you.

A good example of this lies in art appreciation. There is no reason why understanding Impressionism should not give you the ability to appreciate pre-Columbian art as well. The insights and wisdoms of one discipline *should* generalize into others. So many collectors assemble a truly eclectic series of objects, and the great-hearted and truly loving may have a most unusual assortment of friends, though not all of them will necessarily get along with one another. But that is the nature of love: It begins as a twig of desire but, if allowed to grow, you can eventually attach a hammock to it, so to speak. It will then support *you* and let you climb out to where others reside, on their separate branches of desire.

You can now see why a whim not allowed to mature can be so self-defeating. Whims and desires in turn influence an entity's overall intent: They feed it, nourish it, and help it adapt to the realities of the time period in which it seeks fulfillment. Thus, it is quite important to deal with your smallest whims and impulses, for these are the means by which your overall life-intent makes contact with the here-and-now. Think of the light stroking of a snake's tongue or an insect's feelers, testing the environment so that the larger organism behind them may know how best to proceed.

The ice-cream cone may remind our scientist that he has been somewhat neglectful of his family. The monk may be given cause to wonder if giving in to his desire for ice cream will really cast him into the bowels of Hell. And lo! Suddenly the ice cream is no longer the issue.

Let's say I want a specific goal in life, but my Grander Self has something else planned for me. How can I know that I'm working toward my real destination?

As your life changes, so will your specific goals—but the *overall* intent for which you came into this life remains more or less the same. Meanwhile, it is perfectly all right to put effort into any given goal or direction.

Let us say that you entered upon this life to express compassion and love—but in a discriminating manner. In adjacent lives, you may have loved indiscriminately, and someone may have taken your love and used it the wrong way, without giving *you* approval and appreciation. So this time, you are careful to give your love where it is deserved, using it to encourage the best in others as well as in yourself.

You may, as a young child, have quite a few pets and later, many dear friends. Yet no matter how much effort you put into a friendship or a marriage, it will often dissolve, for whatever reason—perhaps people move away; perhaps someone dies. If you feel your efforts are futile, it's usually because you're putting energy into the *means* and not into the goal itself.

This is why we counsel whittling to many of you. For example, if you believe that a house in the country is your highest goal, you may find your house-buying efforts blocked—or worse, not enjoy your house in the country once you get it. It would have behooved you to have whittled *why* you wanted that house in the country, because it could very well be—and often is—a symbol for you.

What is the nature of personal destiny, and how can I choose the highest and best for myself?

Your personal destiny is very much like a hike through the woods: The angle and direction of your approach is constantly changing, relative to your final goal. Your overall intent, which is normally chosen between lives, can be accessed by taking a piece of paper. Write down in a column what your highest goods are. Often, they will not be the top of the mountain where you are actually headed, but trail markers, you might say, to steer you on your way.

To use a different analogy, think of the highest goals you can envision now—this minute—as bright stars in he constellation of your personal destiny. The shape of the overall constellation is not always obvious from the stars that mark it: It takes imagination to see the Big Dipper as a Great Bear. But you can be sure that like a shotgun blast, the "scatter pattern" of your highest goals more or less brackets the region of your personal destiny. It is so worthwhile and necessary a goal that you are given more than one bullet with which to hit the target that it presents to you. And in that sense, every goal you can write down is itself a means to an end—a pellet or arrow that you must fire off, so as to clearly mark your target destiny, which your life's task it is to investigate more closely.

Now, as I have said elsewhere, it may be that you have more than one job to fulfill—more than one destiny—in any one life: As a child, your destiny may be to love and comfort an ailing grandparent; as an adult, to teach others the proper exercise of love and to bring children into the world; and as an oldster, to develop yourself, to read and learn so that you bring back to your Grander Self as many goodies as possible from this lavish gourmet supermarket called physical reality!

This is why I emphasize the importance of writing down what your goals are here and now, *today.* Pay no heed to what you *should* be aiming for, to what a saint or Nobel Prize laureate would aim for, to what your parents, gurus, or lovers might see as *their* highest goals. No matter how seemingly selfish or sleazy or insignificant your goals, write them down and recognize them for what they are! For there is no point in marking time, assuming that your destiny will not manifest itself for another twenty years or more.

Whatever your personal destiny for today, you are on its track right now, even as we speak. And there is no time to waste, especially if you realize that yet another destiny may be waiting to lay claim to your time and energy once this one is safely put to rest.

Now for the second part of your question: If you can trust that your destiny will be the highest it can be, you will automatically be led to your personal mountain top via the most comfortable and direct route.

There are different destinies for each individual; there is room for all of you to fulfill yourselves. The steps to reach it are three: Trust that your highest destiny is there, as a beacon, before you; Expect it to be fed to you piecemeal; Ask to be led. And you will be led—and you will find and recognize that which you have been seeking!

Then if I have trouble getting what I want, that may not represent my true inner goals?

You may, on occasion, buy something that looked wonderful in the store and be crushingly disappointed with it once you get it home. Basically, your desire has satisfied itself, and your overall intent has taken an important course correction.

It is just as important to learn what you do *not* want—what you can do without—as it is to better your tastes and precise-ify your desires. And so, when your cherished hat does not look so good in your home mirror, when the book you bought with such interest sleeps unread on the shelf, do not berate yourself for being frivolous and impractical. You are learning!

A baby reaches out for what she thinks she wants—as an example of what she will later attain as an adult. You can hand that baby a piece of plastic worth exactly nothing in terms of dollars and cents, yet in terms of her *learning*, it may be worth a good deal.

Your archaeologists spend time excavating rotten wood, fragments of clay, and other objects with no intrinsic worth in themselves, for what they can reveal about long-past civilizations. Just so, almost all experience—including love!—is handed to you not for its intrinsic worth, but for its learning value.

A short attention span guarantees that the child will experience a wide range of stimuli in any given time period. So, for adults, is boredom a goad or signal to move on, to enrich your life by—usually—the nearest means possible. But if you have made your environs barren and quiet, you may have to make some major changes in order to fulfill your whim. Whether you live in the Mojave Desert seriously affects the ease with which you can satisfy your desire for an ice-cream cone. And yet, your larger intent—to return to the stimulation of a large city—might manifest itself in just such a craving.

Whims and desires are tricky, meant to lead you on paths and in directions you might not otherwise have "rationally" selected. Even a sailing ship determined to go north must bow to the realities of wind and tide and steer a zigzag course, tacking and jibing to achieve its chosen harbor. And so, any single life entails virtually billions of tiny but vital course corrections. Just as your steering wheel must turn fully if you are not to wind up in the ditch, so must you be willing to pull over, as it were, when the spirit moves you. It is important to trust your trivial whims as the antennae of a larger and more serious purpose—for that very trust, being a form of belief, will strengthen the connection and make your course corrections a little less violent.

To continue that analogy, it would be tragic if the desire to turn left, if unfulfilled, were suddenly to manifest itself several miles later and lead you to crash into a wall. But such can be the effect of any phantom desire reawakened—usually, now—when sensory and other circumstances reproduce themselves exactly. This is how primal therapy attains its goals: by uncovering ghost impulses and recreating the circumstances under which they can finally fulfill and, thus, discharge themselves. But the far less complex way of trusting your impulses—trusting them to lead you wisely *and to evolve on their own*—would make much such therapy quite unnecessary.

C. S. Lewis [in *The Great Divorce*] uses the metaphor of a man with a lizard on his shoulder for the kind of sinner who keeps his sin with him simply because it is familiar. Yet once the sinner lets his compulsion evolve, it becomes—in Lewis's image, now—a white horse that carries its transformed rider swiftly into the higher foothills of Heaven.

A fine example of course correction, if ever I heard one!

8

Returning to Your Grander Self: The Near-Death Experience and Other "Ends" of Life

• *The metaphysics of AIDS* • *Death as a statement about the preceding life* • *What really happens during the Near-Death Experience* • *Discarnate "helpers" who greet the dying* • *Effect of death upon the survivors* • *Why ghosts and hauntings are comparatively rare* • *The* ka *and* ba *of ancient Egypt: expansion and realignment of the personality after death* • *The personality that was Hitler*

Why does AIDS afflict mostly gays in the U.S., but mostly heterosexuals in Africa?

As I am sure you are aware, AIDS is affecting *both* gays and heterosexuals in this country, as well as elsewhere. If you view any single incarnation from the Grander Self's vantage point and not in linear cause-and-effect terms, then different details come to greater prominence.

AIDS causes many of its victims to die at a young age, often in the prime of life. But many in the gay community and many of your sexually active heterosexuals deeply fear middle age, for they conceive that wrinkles and gray hair will deny them access to the most desirable partners. And is AIDS not seen as partly the result of promiscuity—of having many, many sexual partners? Even among those who are *not* sexually active, promiscuity is often seen as enviable.

It is very rare today for anyone to die of a "traditional" venereal disease such as syphilis or gonorrhea. There is no reason why anyone must be sick, unless you are trying to dramatize something, for disease is almost always a dramatization of some inward conflict or cross-purpose within the psyche. And there are as many of *those* as there are diseases in your medical textbooks.

Now, if a friend claimed to have died of the Great Pox in an earlier life, would your reaction be pity, or envy? Death takes on a different meaning in hindsight; and I am not minimizing any kind of tragedy when I say that any relatively novel death will always attract a remarkable number of souls who—knowing that they must dis-incarnate one way or another—opt for a relatively new means.

You have couples who wish to marry and, knowing they can do so only once—to each other, at least—choose to do so under rather bizarre and memorable circumstances: while skydiving, in the nude, or under water. Such options for nuptials have become available only recently, thanks to advances in your technology and sense of humor. It is no accident that a proportionately small but locally numerous number of individuals have rushed to make their transitions in distinctly 20th-century ways: by A-bomb in Japan, by airplane crash in various locales, and now by AIDS—which to a degree has taken up the slack of those venereal diseases that respond to penicillin.

Why does the Black Death no longer rage across continents? Because it no longer has any "takers." Again, I do not wish to minimize the agony of those who allowed that disease to carry them away, but do wish to underscore that they chose it in preference to some other means of dis-incarnation.

Most of you who recall "past" or adjacent lives have little trouble recalling your mode of death, simply because death has a mnemonic value. One recalls the "message" inherent in any particular means of passing. This is why Krishna strongly defends public execution in the *Bhagavad-Gita*, and why so many capital punishments of the past were so tediously—and excruciatingly—symbolic. On a deeper level, your torturers and executioners realized the game they were playing. And even when you choose an undignified, painful, or shameful death or one that causes great grief and anxiety to those around you, still you are choosing according to the *same set of rules* "followed" by those who die peaceably in their sleep at the age of 102.

Each nation has its own favored method of suicide—every state and region of your country, even. So, if you look carefully, does each have its statistically higher causes of death. I leave it to your psychologists to chart the deep correlations between "cause" of death and one's strongest fears and priorities—and to show how the former is almost invariably influenced by the latter.

Is the AIDS epidemic trying to teach us any specific lessons?

Here are three different scenarios that can open the way to AIDS. One is, "If I share my body indiscriminately with others, then perhaps it is not truly mine. Therefore, I will withdraw from it some of my inner protective energy."

Another: "I need drugs to keep my body at bay. It is not something I wish to remain in for a long time. It is a prison to me. Therefore, I need some sure means of exiting the body." Or, "Society looks down on me because of my background or sexual preference, my race or income, my taste in music or where I live. Therefore, instead of seeking the worth I intuitively know is mine, I accept the judgment of the society of which I see myself a victim—and I will come down with something so that it will be *forced* to deal with me and pay attention."

If you define yourself too narrowly, you open yourself to disease, simply because you are cutting down on your own versatility. You are saying, "I am monodimensional." Like a creature that stands on one leg, you are easy to topple. If you stand on two legs, you have better balance. If you stand on three, like a tripod, not even an earthquake can push you over.

One of the lessons of being incarnate is to balance yourself so that the foundations of your pride, the support of your self-esteem, will not be too rigidly defined, as in "If I am not young and comely or part of the establishment, then I am nothing."

Actually, I was talking more in terms of society at large—the people who aren't at risk for AIDS.

For those apparently not at risk for AIDS, the lesson is that you too *are* at risk if you make similar mistakes!

Originally, members of the gay community were at risk, then drug addicts; now those who engage in sex for money and those who are promiscuous in the heterosexual community. The categories of those at risk will continue to spread until and unless you, as a species, look more closely for what *identifies* you with your brothers and sisters, as opposed to what separates you from them. Too often, your civilizations have divided themselves into various classes or subsections. Where there is separation, there is the possibility of stagnation: Energy cannot flow healthily within a society where certain groups are made to feel separate. The lesson of AIDS is that all must come together to stop the spread of a *common* disease.

I should explain that viruses, by their very nature, serve as the shepherds and prompters of physical species. They hurry certain plants and animals to ecological niches where they can best survive, and they inhibit the growth of life forms that would otherwise overcome Nature herself. The goal of Nature is diversity: She wishes to display the widest possible variety of divergent subspecies. Where one life form threatens to overwhelm all others, the scythe of virus is invited to prune back excessive numbers of the offending species and allow other life forms their rightful place in the sun.

Nature does not mourn the loss of individuals, but the reduction of diversity. Within any natural habitat, the kaleidoscope of species should be as various, outrageous, and provocatively disparate as the exploded rubble of a natural history museum. And wherever one species would hog the scene, there comes a most profound shakeup that upsets the monotonous pattern and re-introduces to the kaleidoscope a new set of shards that can grow into fresh patterns. A species is not fulfilled by numbers and survival alone, not when its members become too monotonously similar. Viruses are built-in regulators and scene changers, serving not Nature as much as *the species themselves*, ensuring that those individual species distribute themselves and evolve and (which is sometimes most important!) retreat from the territories they have found most congenial. And almost invariably, the intent and basic mandate of any virus is to prune back the more shapeless incoherences of any one species, such that surrounding life may enjoy the breathing space of wider opportunity.

Your own human race is not exempt from this basic rule. Rain forests support their indigenous life forms better than they can support those who cut them down. If the rain forests fall, your planet is naked—but I say, your Earth will preserve her modesty. AIDS is preserving Africa for life forms who live there, and South America is next. AIDS cases are erupting there, but because the affected countries wish to be beyond reproach, they're not reporting them.

What is not acknowledged, spreads. And those at the cutting edge of the deforestation visit prostitutes on Saturday nights. Your rain forests will be able to return once the cutting is arrested.

Through a Near-Death Experience, can a person learn his or her purpose for being here?

Yes and no. Your purpose in this life is like your reason for going to the supermarket. If you are wise and efficient, you seldom go to the market for one set of items—only for paper towels or green beans, or every time you need a carrot or a stick of butter. No, you save up your needs and make a shopping list. And when you incarnate, you don't go for one purpose only—imagine the waste of growing a body from scratch for one single purpose!

Now, many of you have Near-Death Experiences to check in with your Grander Self. It is a bit like calling home from the market and saying, "Honey, I'm sure I forgot something. Oh, yes—I'll go back for some coffee!"

Frequently, after such an experience, you find you have more energy to "spend," and there is more room than you knew in your shopping cart. Halfway through the aisles of life, you might remember a recipe from an adjacent existence and want to pick up some extra ingredients—for that is basically what you are all doing here: picking up ingredients.

In a Near-Death Experience, you experience a higher degree of free will than is usually granted. Why have you been given free will? Basically, so that you may use it to converse with your own Grander Self.

That is a long and loaded statement, and you can all unravel it at your own leisure.

Are only a few people allowed to remember their Near-Death Experiences?

Many who are resuscitated know perfectly well that they *will* be resuscitated, and so use the "downtime" of the body for rest. They intuitively know this is not the end, and so remain . . . not earthbound, but rather "bodybound." They simply do not project outward with the same kind of gusto and exuberance that other Near-Death Experiencers experience.

A short answer, but a true one.

Is it usual for older people to be able to see non-physical entities?

It is not unusual in the least.

To a very large degree, people of *all* ages perceive a great many more entities than you would expect. During the prime of physical life, however, the focus on earthly life is usually so narrow—intense, you might say—that such "extraneous" beings are swept aside from conscious awareness.

You can see a good analogy to this in a father who is intent on balancing his checkbook or fixing the carburetor on his lawnmower. Silently and discreetly, his children pad through the room or garage. And so deep is his concentration that he is wholly unaware of their presence. He is much less likely to notice visitors who are not in their physical bodies!

In very young children, and again in the elderly, this precise concentration lapses to a large degree—but not out of inability, however! Genetically, the young child is programmed to maintain a few ties to the non-physical realm. Before your era of modern medicine, children stood a fairly good chance of not surviving to adolescence. It would have been cruel to return them to non-physical reality with no preparation at all; and so, historically, children have kept a few lines of perception and focus open to other realities, almost as a means of insurance. This is one reason why your human species takes so long to mature—both physically and psychologically. It is also why children are more likely to recall adjacent lives, to see "spirits," engage in odd practices not sanctioned by their parents—and why, also, such ESP abilities tend to shut down after adolescence has come to an end. At this stage, a young adult has more or less committed him- or herself to physical reality for the duration, and is focused rather precisely onto the challenges of the physical here-and-now.

But when that same personality's life work is nearing its fulfillment, it will seek extra stimulation in familiar realms beyond the physical. Even as it dusts off its inner senses and stretches its long-abandoned abilities, it will learn to perceive— and come to comfortable terms with—entities of other realities from whom it has been temporarily and necessarily estranged, and with whom it is now renewing acquaintances. Such visions imply a kind of *health*, then, and do not smack of senility.

How do we choose when to die? Or do our Grander Selves decide to remove us from physical reality?

When you've done as much as you can, your physical body shuts down—yes, dies. Very simply, you do not die as much as you fall silent, when you are convinced you have nothing more to communicate, when you have presented all you possibly can and feel—emotionally, now—that your colleagues have turned away to examine what you have given them, or to examine other gifts given by others. You've spoken your piece and, therefore, need speak no longer.

If death is our choice, why are we afraid of it?

Good question—you tell me!

I'm not afraid of death as much as the pain of dying.

Pain is a distraction, you see, from what you want in life. You cannot go out and fulfill yourself if you are in pain. Nor can you *be* yourself: On the rack, you may sign a false confession. Recognizing that no one wishes to speak with you any more is indeed painful. But some of you are proud enough to silence yourselves before others turn away. Occasionally, those afraid they will not be listened to are audacious enough to bite off their own tongues—and it hurts!

You are afraid of death if you feel you have not done or said all that you need to in life. That is the soul's fear: that the energy you need to express yourself as an individual will run out before that which you have to express. Pain is finite, silence is forever. "I'll have another song to sing, when the Angel of Death says 'Shhh!'" Is that not your fear—of being struck silent?

But on a biological level, you are not so worried. Those who have who have confronted death and gone through close encounters of the worst kind know that death is no big thing. It is "Oh, look! Here comes the express train!" Bang!

When your voice is no longer needed in physical existence, then you die. But also, you fall silent because you have perfected your song. And so, you close out your out-of-town tryout here on Earth and are ready to take your show on the celestial road.

Are there other places where we will be listened to?

Oh, yes! Other theatres—of operation, you might say. You are now undergoing rehearsals, to learn what makes an audience laugh and applaud.

Anyone incarnate is working to upgrade his or her skills, that other gigs may be attempted—and when you are still on the road, you can afford to bomb. Of course, there is no Great White Way in the sky where you tap-dance for eternity. But when you have perfected your skills, you can display them to others without worrying that anyone will steal them away from you—because you are the source of those skills.

I know of several people who were critically ill, but otherwise in complete touch with reality, who spoke of the presence of loved ones who were "dead." When we approach death, do our loved ones come to help us make the transition?

Quite true. When you transit, ones who have preceded you may make an extra effort and, by putting on the likenesses you knew them by in life, come as midwives to attend the emergence of your spirit from the comparatively sluggish womb of Earth. But as you approach physical death, *you* make an equally robust effort to adapt—and if you perceive "departed" others, that is to *your* credit as much as it is to theirs. In a very real sense, your loved ones *are with you at all times*, always "there"—even though you may each decide to focus attention elsewhere to facilitate your independent development. The grave is hardly a barrier, merely a discreet dumpster for abandoned bodies. You put your body to one side, much as you would a suit grown too small for you. And just as a man in bathing trunks can be expected to behave differently than when he is decked out in white tie and tails, so does the lack of a body predispose you to certain amusements that might otherwise have escaped you.

When a physical personality dies, what happens to its non-physical components—and to other, still-living personalities on the spectrum of the Grander Self?

You ask two separate questions . . .

In your terms, the dying personality dies to a higher sphere of influence, even as your scientists imagine that energized electrons are boosted to ascending shells around the atomic nucleus.

Think of your astronauts, who see the Earth more clearly from space and feel a wonder and affection for it that they do not sense when they stand directly upon it. Similarly, when you die, you will be simultaneously removed from—and more in touch with—the Entire Source of your being.

As for other individual parts of this Grander Entity, think of the dandelion: Just because one seed blows away, that does not mean the other seeds must lose their grip. They will ripen and venture forth in their own time. In one sense, there is greater energy available to the "surviving" aspects—but I must complicate that statement by explaining that each of you has died *several* times in this life! It sounds like a paradox, but it is not. Think back in your life to when you narrowly averted an accident, recovered from a serious illness, or felt a sense of doom and saw no exit from a life that was dark, lonely, and cold. Of course, the accident did not occur; you recovered; things changed. But in a sense, a probable you *did* die in those alternate circumstances, taking with it—and away from the "you" that survived—a number of negativities, so you could begin the rest of your life with fewer burdens and anxieties.

Any large-intent event is rehearsed in some way, either in a dream, in a probability, or as a split-second calculation at the beginning of the event itself. The life that flashes in front of a dying person's eyes is like a high-speed computer analysis. The self, thinking that it may die, reviews the circumstances leading up to the instant of death: "Does dis-associating from the physical fulfill my intents at this point in time?" In short, the individual is doing a spot calculation to see whether the death is justified, whether it "computes."

Do dying individuals bequeath energy to their relatives, as at the end of the novel Watership Down?

Not in the sense of a *direct* transfer of energy. A new-dead individual needs plenty of energy to re-orient himself in the after-death environment. The cellular extinguishings of the body release energies of different sorts, but not the kind that neighboring bodies could use directly.

What does happen is that dying individuals send forth two different kinds of signals. The short-term signal acts as a klaxon, a warning to other life forms that danger is present, and is amplified drastically when a being dies in pain and fear.

The longer-term signal is far more peaceful and wakens certain impulses in those who have chosen to remain "behind." Just as certain angles of light and length of day trigger blooming among plants and spawning among animals, so does the event of a death—even a death of which you are not consciously aware—cause quickening and germination in certain parts of the psyche.

On a most obvious level, the death of a giant in any human endeavor—say, Picasso—will encourage the growth and devel-opment of others in the same field who, during the master's life-time, might have been afraid to compete with him. There is a natural tact and reticence, among humans especially, not to challenge the old masters at their own game.

The same kind of succession occurs, of course, when a large tree topples in the forest and admits light to its own seedlings. So does a king bequeath his crown and kingdom to his prin-ces; so does a departing leader in any realm send out a clarion challenge to the young that the field is again open for compe-tition. And thus at times, when reading of a stranger's death, you will find a strange exhilaration—which is of course muffled and camouflaged with guilt, should the deceased be known to you personally.

Thus, some of your societies chose that their kings should be killed each year, literally as "seed corn" to encourage the growth of other talents and abilities in the region. And of course, such a practice was not seen as terribly cruel once reincarnation was factored into the picture.

I understand that an individual has his or her own reasons for choosing an early death. But the death of John F. Kennedy or John Lennon becomes a mass event, with a profound effect on thousands of other people. In such a case, what are the underlying issues involved?

It is difficult to fully articulate the exquisite cooperation that goes into the creation of your everyday life. Quite literally, the meshings and confluence that assure that all of you can sail on the same seas and yet achieve your individually desired harbors require a kind of mental physics that would put the complexities of quantum mechanics to shame.

So it is with death. Quite often, you will become attached to certain behavior patterns in yourself that, on a higher level, you would like to be rid of. And yet—out of affection or habit, nostalgia or fear—these patterns are retained. In such a case, often your Grander Self will arrange with another individual on his or her way out of physical reality to act as a catalyst to help you "take out the garbage," as it were, and relieve you of your ambiguous burden.

Not that you load your own private hassles onto the bent shoulders of those in physical pain, who are about to die. Rather, the very mourning process that one undergoes for other individuals of whom one is fond acts as a kind of solvent for the psyche, allowing it—during those periods of grief and emotional upheaval—to slough off old layers in habits that have outlived their usefulness.

Those of you who would get rid of a bad habit—smoking, overweight, even persistent mental patterns—would be wise to hold an imaginary wake or funeral for it, with as much conscious symbolism and ritual as you can muster without feeling foolish. This is the main reason behind some of the more extravagant funeral customs practiced by different societies around the globe. Into the open grave or pyre or Viking longboat are flung not only flowers, but many small but no longer welcome attributes of the self that the survivors prefer to survive without.

And so, you can expect that the death of anyone important to you personally will somehow leave you lightened, cleansed, and purified to the degree that you *yourself* have been dissatisfied and desiring change—this is in addition to the signal-of-death that most entities broadcast, as I explained before. But do not feel that these inward passings-away leave your total being any the less. Think of them as dead leaves, discarded during one of your personal emotional autumns, so that the healthy buds and new shoots that you have dimly dreamt of shall have room to grow and expand the outline of your being as a whole.

Are ghosts and poltergeists more likely to manifest near coordinate points?

Many different types of phenomena come under your rubric of *ghosts*; it is like saying "marine life."

One category of ghost is where an individual has died violently, and a certain amount of emotion has soaked into the death environment. Like the flash from an explosion, this "ghost" is a suspended moment, a strong image of an event—often a death, but not always.

Hauntings often happen when you sight the bleedthrough of a parallel event. Where one individual sees a ghost and another doesn't, each person is in a different vibratory area.

Spirits are not normally earthbound, in your terms. Upon your death, you can maneuver in simultaneous time, so—from your perspective, now—your single identity is able to exist in several places at once. A seemingly earthbound ghost is usually part of the baggage a departing individual left behind, and in due course, its Greater Self will come by and pick it up.

As for poltergeists, they are constructs exteriorized from within the psyche. They tend to occur where previous emotional energies have been focused—and projected. Many of you have been responsible for "instant poltergeists," hauntings that lasted only a minute or two. When an object you *know* you put away safely, vanishes and reappears in the damnedest place, this is a mini-poltergeist at work.

That process is normal and not to be feared: If you can dematerialize the car keys, you can work on dematerializing unwanted thought-forms, habits, fears, and paranoias. And it is healthier to do that yourself than to ask the universe to do it for you!

Departed spirits don't seem to manifest in physical reality very often. What prevents them from doing so?

There are automatic levels of separation.

Strictly speaking, there is nothing to stop your 7-year-old from wandering into a college lecture hall and sitting down to a lecture on advanced calculus. But most 7-year-olds would rather be out playing baseball than listening to something that, to them, makes no sense.

Yes, it is all one curriculum, but there are different stages of understanding—and radically different "classrooms" to be entered, once you have graduated beyond the body. Certain classrooms come before others; and one necessity for any kind of learning is to avoid wasting your time by prematurely overspecializing in any one endeavor. You may bemoan the fact that children have such short attention spans, but they are programmed that way, in order to experience a wide range of ground in as short a time as possible. Later, having accelerated themselves through a number of disciplines, they can specialize.

Now, those who have passed beyond your physical level *may* choose to return and specialize in contact with the "living." But after having examined all their new options, they seldom view manifesting in their previous home base as terribly rewarding, especially since they can do so more easily in their new realm. Even if they still identify with their old physical body, they find themselves—because of their different vibrational rate—less able to get someone else's physical body in gear. They can sit in the car, you might say, but can no longer make it run. Except by controlling a weak incarnate spirit via resonance, they cannot possess or "drive" surviving bodies. Even the largely hallucinatory body that a ghost or revenant constructs to make itself visible is mainly for show, and of little practical use. Progression seems far more tempting!

Susy Smith's **The Book of James** *states that because of "evolutionary soul progression," reincarnation in body after body in subsequent lives is unnecessary. One life is all the soul needs to learn its lessons and afterward, it continues to evolve on its own.*

Needless to say, this contradicts everything I've read about reincarnation. Do we live life after life, or not?

Both! It is true that you live only one life on Earth and then continue to evolve after physical death. It is equally true that you live lives so numerous that it is sometimes hard to keep track of them all. Too many of your metaphysicians have traced only one modality of after-life development, which would be akin to trying to pinpoint the location of an explosion by following only one of the chunks of matter that it expelled. Such a course of research would take you rather far afield from where the action is—or was.

As I have suggested, upon death the personality expands itself and is able to follow several lines of development *simultaneously*. The earthly personality continues to refine itself, for much the same reason that you hold still for a photographer—so that a vivid image of you can be preserved for future reference. In a sense, then, you are destined to become a quite living "portrait" of your earthly self, which will retain its own individuality and recognizable characteristics. On yet another level, however, your personality begins to "climb back up" the Oversoul or Grander Self of which it is a part.

This process is what your Near-Death Experiencers recall as passing through a tunnel, toward a Source of most dazzling brilliance. Imagine someone becoming aware of first his finger, then his hand, then his arm and shoulder, and you will have a rough approximation of what goes on when a portion of the recently incarnate psyche goes "upstream," experiencing the various levels of the Self that gives it life. It may not make a complete journey and may well return "down" to bud off into another incarnation; for from the Grander Self's and reincarnating soul's point of view, *all* incarnations are seen as simultaneous, parallel, contemporary. The leaves on a tree or the spines of a sea urchin are all present at once, though some may be more recent than others, and comparatively few of them ever touch or intersect with one another.

And so it is that the Egyptians postulated two spirits for the deceased, the *ka* and the *ba*: one corresponding to the portion of the personality that retains its earthly trappings, and the other corresponding to that portion—or version, really—that evolves "upward" toward its soul-source and then often comes back, invigorated and re-energized, to emerge joyfully into flesh once again.

You should not find this odd, much less threatening. In everyday life, you are able to cook, eat, dress yourself, play, work, and devote yourself to a myriad of different tasks and challenges, including dream-state activities—all within any given 24-hour period. Now, when time is infinitely compressed to the point where you could accurately say that it no longer exists at all—or rather, when there is *all the time you require*—it is quite possible to do any number of things simultaneously.

If you were to instill your consciousness in your breath and then breathe out, it might appear that your identity was dissipating into some kind of nebulous Nirvana. And yet, who drew in that breath to begin with? Whenever a portion of identity seems lost, there is always a greater Self, a grander Identity, who occasioned the "loss"—and in Whom that scrap of identity is safely preserved.

Imagine a living photo album, or a number of versions of yourself, "taken" at different ages and all equally alive, and you will begin to grasp how deeply and thoroughly your Grander Self cherishes you—both for what you are and have been, and for what, in other dimensions and realms, you may become. Even as a photographer takes more than one snapshot of his chosen subject, so does your curiosity require more than one "picture" of physical reality to satisfy it. If someone blocks your view in one existence, he or she will move in an adjacent one, so that you can finally make your shot or take your picture.

Does Adolf Hitler intend to reincarnate in the near future? If so, what will his life be like?

The Hitler energy is, in a sense, continuing the counter-productive paradox that he assumed in life.

I say "the Hitler energy," for this man, this individual, drew to himself the ambitions and frustrations of an entire people, identifying as strongly with his historical role as he did with his trappings and perquisites of power. That symbolic overlay is now a grievous hindrance to his progress in any direction. In other words, his status and his identity became mixed up, such that he could not recall where his personal sphere of influence ended.

In the state he now finds himself, he is still, you could say, in a bunker—assuming that he is under attack and being sought out for punishment *because he is the embodiment of the German ambition*. To re-state that: he assumes he is being revenged upon, being singled out as the representative and instigator of war—again, quite simply, because he will not drop the role he wore in life.

He has also fragmented himself, in a way that is roughly similar to those who wish to investigate new experiences—but here, the entity has been diminished and dismembered, not augmented, by such fragmentation. Just as the Germans—and other retreating armies throughout history—have buried plunder in various places to protect it, so has the Hitler energy, out of a sense of self-defense, "buried" itself and gone to ground in a number of protective bunkers. And because the basic posture is fearful, not assertive, it is resistant to any learning.

The entity feels compelled to mull over the pieces of the puzzle it brought with it, then, and will not accept any new pieces—much less new borders or new possible solutions—that might hasten a resolution of past conflicts and conundrums.

Am I saying, then, that the Hitler energy is more than merely human, closer to a gestalt such as many Grander Selves claim themselves to be? No—it merely took these trappings unto itself, and *believes* that its accumulated purpose is still alive and active, when in reality it is not. It is a human core, a core of discarnate human energy, embedded in the center of a host of thought-forms and inert trappings from which others have long since withdrawn their energies.

Think of a tree, bristling with bare and lifeless branches culled from other trees, with only a narrow green heart that is shadowed over by its own welter of dead foliage. Such a spiritual tumbleweed, though fixed and not tumbling, is the Hitler energy. Dante intuitively understood this kind of defensive, hysterically self-protective being that covers itself over with the beliefs of others, and imagined a rough approximation of such beings in his Wood of the Suicides. I said "approximation" there, and my metaphors are approximations as well.

The posthumous lesson of the Hitler energy is simply this: Allow to drop away any external concepts or ambitions *that have been placed on you by others*—by parents, by society, by lovers and co-workers.

To paraphrase Dickens, you risk wearing the laurels you forged in life, unless you let your crown drop its old foliage, even as the living laurel does, and sprout new buds better suited for a New Age.

9

Reincarnational Configurations:
The Ultimate Life Form

• Relationship of a Grander Self to its incarnate components • The concept of adjacent—not "past"—lives • Specific reincarnational recall, versus inner knowing • James's relationship with other Grander Selves • How Grander Selves manifest themselves, perceive humans, and pass their "time" • The Grander Self as banyan tree • How the personality seeks its own symmetrical fulfillment—in life, and out of it • The inevitable self-fulfillment of being • When reincarnation finally ends

James, how long has your physical body been dead?

As if you couldn't notice, *this* one is still kicking! Other of my physical bodies have been dead for as long as—in your terms—30,000 years.

From my point of view, therefore, how long a body of mine has been "mold'ring in the grave" is almost meaningless—because on the one hand, I can monitor our friend's sensations, his ambitions, his apprehensions about his checking account . . . while on the other, I can pull back and orchestrate—I mean that quite literally—his experience with that of my other incarnated selves; just as you, turning the dial or the controls upon your stereo, could modulate individual instruments, individual signals, to produce a larger whole. I am not using that analogy frivolously. Your Oversouls—or as I prefer to call them, Grander Selves—are balancing you, as various incarnate individuals, in a larger symphony. Each of you is, you might say, both instrument and player of a given part in a symphony in which you participate. Nor do you play in only one orchestra! When you leave here today, each of you will go and play in individual orchestras around the country and, indeed, around the world.

That analogy is closer to what it is all about, because the symphonies—the Grander Selves' plays—are never fixed. They are "improv" all the way. Maybe some of you thought that your part was over, and so you were about to lay down your violin or, in this case, your bodies. Your Grander Self said, "Sorry, we have another movement for you. Let's take it again —not from the top, but from where you left off before."

But now, because your Grander Self has caught your eye, you are watching the baton. You who have returned from the Near-Death Experience know how to play better, you might say—and I mean that as a pun! You know how to *play* better.

I'm a little confused. Are you living in *Tam or* with *Tam?*

I am living *through* him, as you live through, let's say, your fingers. Your fingers are your way of feeling what the world is all about, and of manipulating your world. You use your fingers both to *take* information and *provide* information, as via a typewriter or via the piano.

I am learning through him, even as you learn through your fingers. As you know, it is not your finger who learns. Rather, your brain learns to interpret what your finger is sensing. *You*, however, are living, learning fingers with wisdom and cunning of your own, which only augment the powers of your Grander Self.

Each of you has two arms, two legs, two eyes, but we Grander Selves are not so restricted. In your terms, we might have four eyes, if that did the job better—if we were really into vision. Or if we wished to sense without eyes, we might have none whatsoever. Some colleagues of mine prefer to incarnate in tribal societies because they can achieve their balance—their symphony—quite well using only, let's say, percussion instruments. A rare example, but it does occur.

Are we more likely to be influenced by our most recent past lives than by lives that we lived thousands of years ago?

It all depends. Rather than using the term *past lives*, I suggest you conceive of what I call *adjacent existences*. That prompts a more accurate picture of how incarnation really operates.

Imagine yourself at a marina. In the berth next to you may be a kayak or an Egyptian craft from 3,000 B.C. that chooses to sail on the morning tide. Later that afternoon, a World War II PT Boat may dock there. And so, the lifetime closest to you *psychologically* is not necessarily the closest one chronologically, in your terms of time.

Imagine a roll of pennies, each bearing a different consecutive date from 1800 to 1995, and stacked in chronological order. Some exuberant, youthful hand knocks over the stack. The coins roll and scatter, coming to rest everywhere—atop each other, next to one another, heads up or down. 1896 may be right beside 1930. 1815 may lie atop 1964. 1918 may have rolled off under the bureau and never be heard from again. And so it is with your lives, your incarnations. Your Oversoul is constantly rattling the spare change in its pocket, and so your "present" life is constantly coming into contact with other past *and* future lives that may be quite distant in terms of chronological time, but extraordinarily intimate in terms of their psychological presence.

Yes, occasionally two coins do stick together. This is the source of the morbid obsessions that sometimes come to the fore during a past-life regression. Your concept of free will prevents you from becoming "stuck" to any particular future life, even though you may well get bogged down in *this* life by seeking a protective—thus restrictive—future for yourself. Yet once you realize that you have total free will to choose which "past" lives to berth next to and be influenced by, then much of your fear of past traumas will evaporate.

If you retained a fearful memory of every time you died, you would each be a tangle of phobias. The more lives you accumulated, the worse those fears would become. Clearly, this is not the case! "Older" souls are *less* afraid of death, just as the rodeo cowboy who has broken many bones hardly cares if he cracks yet another rib. In the long multi-life run, the *worst* experiences *cast out* fears, whereas in your individual lives, it is frequently just the opposite.

Not all bone-deep wisdom is accurate, and that is why you often agree to inter that so-called "intelligence" with the bones you leave behind.

A psychic once told me I lived in ancient Egypt. Sometimes I feel I ought to travel there to complete the circle, you might say, and sew up any unfinished business.

In a very real sense, any one life is much like a year spent abroad during college—except that the education never stops, the courses are well-nigh endless, and the tuition is virtually free.

Speaking of just *this* life, now, it may be that you went to kindergarten in Cambridge, England. You may have learned to walk in the halls of Harvard, or spoken your first words in a lecture hall at Yale. Does that necessarily mean you must return to any of these places for your Master's? I would say not. You can find wise professors leaving for field trips in rural Africa, so as to learn more than they could at their sophisticated universities.

You live to gain the tools to learn better and more deeply. Just as an artist learns from each new painting, so do you draw breath not only to fill your lungs, but as a form of practice for your next inhalation. Had you never drawn breath in ancient Egypt, you would have found it hard, upon your current birth, to know how to fill your lungs for the first time.

There are no limits to where learning may happen. Some janitors spend more time in lecture halls than any student; yet, not being present at the proper time, they learn nothing of what is taught there. So with your own learning: Know that wherever you live, wherever you walk, happens to be a lecture hall. If you open your ears, you may discover that the lecture has already begun!

I wanted to ask, real briefly, about some of my adjacent lives —what seem to me past lives.

If I were to begin tediously with a given life, it would only have parallels in other "places"—for most people have one or two sidecars or outriggers, you might say, that balance and complement their present personalities. I'd rather give you some of your alternate ways of working out your interests *throughout* your incarnations.

You can envision your current self as, say, the shadow of a basketball or an orange. The orange is three-dimensional; the shadow is two-dimensional. In the same way, you are a four-dimensional shadow of one facet of your Oversoul.

The overall configuration of your present life will show where you fit on the larger circumference of that Grander Self.

Of course, it is impossible to get in touch with your spiritual geometry unless I give you some of the parameters. And here they are—for your case. Pick your own cultures, pick your own centuries, but here comes your Grander Self's main *configuration*.

One of the themes—not so much of your present life as of your intent; but of course, the intent spills into this life— is that of a double agent, one who can work in a given belief system while also working for another . . . not merely trying to aggrandize himself, though that is part of it. In some of your adjacent existences, you play the traitor, the trickster, the mole—in the espionage sense—who shows others that their nations and belief systems are not the only ones that can command respect and allegiance.

I do not prefer the term *lives*, for lives begin and end. *EXISTENCES GO ON FOREVER!!* That, without yelling, is my message: adjacent existences!

Another part of the "Greater You" is very vulnerable. An entire life, or perhaps a major portion of a given life, may be devoted to expressing this. For example, you might be a child who "dies" in infancy or young childhood—totally dependent, totally receptive, drinking it all in, with very little ego to screen out that which enters in. Or you might be a woman or young man, deeply wishing for direct experience without any censoring whatsoever. Hence, on a physical level, you might find yourself being victimized, simply because you have projected the necessary power—responsibility for choice and discrimination—onto someone else.

However, who chooses? Who sits in the theater, saying, "Let's roll the movie!"? You are the instigator, so do not see yourself as powerless. Indeed, no entity does—if it truly did, your rate of suicide would be close to 90 percent. Few commit suicide, for that reason alone: On a deeper level, they know. But when they refuse to listen on that deeper level, they begin listening to the world, as if the world's wisdom were their own.

Okay, that was a second theme, and I'm going to give you three. There are others, of course, but all of them spread out from these three. The third—you'll be amused by this!—is the total conformist who knows that by running the gauntlet of conformity perfectly, he will emerge safely from the other end, even as the bullet knows that if it spirals perfectly along the gun barrel—if it pays its dues—it will suddenly emerge into total freedom.

And so, this is the ballast side of your configuration: the punk who dresses precisely according to fashion; the long-suffering stockbroker; the toiler who stores up good karma; the penitent who atones for not only his or her own sins, but for others'; and the miser of spiritual gains. They add up to another part of your configuration—another prong on the snow-flake, if I may.

I will use *configuration* in future in dealing with people's reincarnational "pasts," so-called! It will shake up others who think of their reincarnations as fixed, as lower apartments on the condominium of the self—on which they have to pay maintenance! And *you* enjoy shaking people up! In this life, that is one of your prongs.

How do these other selves enrich our current life if we can't even remember them?

The answer is simple: You have gut-level knowledge. You know the multiplication table, but have forgotten the third-grade lesson that taught it to you.

That is why your memories of adjacent existences are necessarily dim. You do not need the specifics. You do not care to remember the war in which you learned not to kill. You need not remember the specific individual who taught you the value of forgiveness and loving.

By all means, request and expect that your other past, present, and future existences will meld their knowledge with your own. But let it be an unconscious gut-level knowing, not a barrage of images out of *Masterpiece Theatre*. That will be easier on you—and more graceful in the long run.

How can a person be considered an old soul and yet new to the Earth Plane?

One term I would like to overhaul so you can use it properly is *old soul*. If time is simultaneous, then how can a soul be old?

Which parameter do you use—how long that soul has been on Earth? You can meet relative yo-yos who have reincarnated 50,000 years ago and are coming back for the first time. Those are "old souls" in one sense, but you would not want them operating heavy machinery in your vicinity.

What you think of as an old soul is more like a catamaran with several pontoons, so that this entity is not shaken by winds or heavy surf, but rides steadily. "Old souls" have that kind of placidity. And because they are able to steady themselves with their own multi-dimensional counterparts, they can sense themselves as not alone in the world, not facing challenges totally on their own. When presented with a given conundrum, they immediately assume—on a knowing, gut level—that others are capable of overcoming this difficulty. If the knowledge exists, why should it not be available to them? And lo, they come through!

This kind of knowing faith characterizes old souls. You think such an individual must have lived several lifetimes, piled up lots of good karmic credits, to enjoy such serenity? No: The key is a willingness to acknowledge simultaneous experience happening on other levels of reality and of what you *think of* as time.

That is why you are here now, learning to interpret the signals of triumph, reassurance, and solution that other aspects of yourself, in other bases of reality, are broadcasting.

What's the difference between soul mates and twin souls?

Quite simply, twin souls are part of the same Larger Entity. They tend to "crop up" again and again in a number of adjacent lives—usually in some complementary role. Just as a pliers has two jaws, so often can a Grander Self "grasp" more by employing two of its own offshoots in a kind of pincer movement. The Entity cannot experience all that it wishes or needs to without such bifurcation—yet at the same time, it "specializes" by focusing two of its simultaneous lives on a single fulcrum of endeavor.

Twins souls used to this kind of larger cooperation—or occasionally, opposition and conflict—will tend to run into each other again and again. Lifelong rivals in a given sport, in politics, or the military can often be twin souls. On a deeper level, they recognize one another as part of the same Entity, and thus are inclined to cooperate—or at least, not do one another any lasting damage.

Soul *mates*, on the other hand, are ones who have frequently reincarnated as lovers, spouses, or members of each other's immediate family. Their task, if you wish to call it that, is a lighter one: merely to explore each other and renew an affection that has offshoots in adjacent lives. That "merely" can of course involve offspring, perhaps also a long-term compromise in which these two work out with each other personality defects and other moral shortcomings—*with* each other, because they would not tolerate from an outsider the sort of criticism or advice they accept from a loved one.

Soul mates will, above all, feel a sense of recognition and instant attraction for one another. As you might guess, there can be more than one of them in any one lifetime! It is quite possible for you to meet different members of the opposite sex with whom you have had steamy and satisfying relations—albeit in separate existences. And so now, in your present reunion, it may be difficult for you to choose among soul mates unless your hand is forced by circumstances—as it usually will be, by unanimous consent. A romance novel in which one of the beloveds dies prematurely is a dim echo of the kind of soul mate who has decided to "move on" and make way for someone else.

Soul mates can also manifest themselves as excellent friends. They can also vary in degree, so that—for example—one you have married in four separate adjacent lives will attract you more compellingly than another with whom you have been involved in only one other existence. It is also possible for soul mates to be twin souls, part of the same Larger Entity, though this kind of metaphysical incest is comparatively rare. Usually, the Grander Self prefers to scrape off its barnacles against another's offshoots and to increase its possible interactions by consorting with personalities it has not engendered.

The only danger is that you may be led to believe that your destiny has been cast in some unimaginably distant and forgotten past; and that you are now in the thrall of an attraction that dates back several thousand years. Remember that your *current* affection nourishes these "past" lovers as much as they nourish you, and that matters can always be improved and intensified by giving one another due respect, honor, and support in the here-and-now.

I want to emphasize that such a beloved is hardly chosen for you. *You* do the choosing, and having a soul mate in no way lets you off the hook. By his or her very presence, the soul mate implies that certain challenges are now to be met, certain quirks of pride and self-centeredness ready to be overcome.

You are not puppets in the grip of your own past selves. You are, each of you, the well from which your Grander Self and collateral selves can slake their thirst for growth and experience.

Why do we keep on reincarnating?

Why do you go back to the supermarket? We see you leaving with your arms full of goodies, and lo, a week later, you are back again! Of course, the answer is the same: There are specials!

If you wish to be present when word first reaches Spain of a new land beyond the Azores, you must needs be alive in 1492. Others might prefer to rub elbows with Cromwell, or Charlemagne, or Pericles—which individuals incarnated for relatively brief spans of time. A gold rush can happen only once; your American West can be "conquered" only a single time. And so, the different ages of your world each have their own unique pheromone that attracts incoming souls drawn to the pleasant whiff of those particular circumstances.

Can a Larger Entity begin a reincarnational cycle and then, in the "middle," suddenly realize the venture isn't in its best interests and abort the cycle?

No, because there are certain limitations on the possible negative experiences of any one incarnation.

When a personality decides to become flesh, certain lessons to be learned and certain emotional and gut-level "topics" are selected in advance, before the actual incarnation begins. So from the Grander Self's point of view, there are no surprises. Nothing is sneaked into the incarnate's bag of groceries that the Oversoul did not willingly choose in the first place.

Individuals may bemoan having not as good a lot as their peers. Indeed, they may *seem* to have been shortchanged in terms of what they bring into this life. But these are the accepted rules of the Higher Game, and do not constitute reason enough for the Oversoul to withdraw itself from physical reality.

Your question presupposes a blameless form of suicide—in which, to change analogies, an Oversoul finds the earthly movie not what it paid to see, and so walks out of the theater. Such is not the case! It may be that *individuals* choose to commit suicide; and—not too surprisingly—how serious that offense is depends on their motive. If they select self-annihilation at the end of a long and varied life, to forestall severe inconvenience and physical pain for themselves—or better yet, for others—then *that* particular suicide *may* be entirely blameless. It may, in fact, have been chosen in advance. Before their lives began, many of your ancient Romans chose to die by their own hand, as did many of your samurai and so-called martyrs who went willingly to the axe or gallows rather than compromise the thrust of their overall life-intention.

I am not making a case for suicide, even where it seems condoned by custom. Those who slit their wrists or overdose on pills are directing valuable energy inward against themselves, when the same anger, guilt, and emotional seethe—no matter how unpleasant—could far more *easily* be projected outward to make needed changes in the external environment.

In other words, the despair that leads to suicide is the result of change-impulses directed inward, rather than outward where they belong. Despairing of change within or without, the depressive may feel an impulse to suicide—to break the logjam, as it were. But whenever the individual stumbles so far out of bounds, the Oversoul must, in effect, call a time out and have that personality run the play again—often from the beginning.

I am not saying that suicide is the worst of all unpardonable sins—because none is—or that you will burn in a hell of your own creation as a result of having committed it. I *am* saying that to *whatever* degree you evade the responsibilities and lessons that incarnate life has to grant you, to that degree you are wasting the advantages and opportunities inherent in consciousness itself.

Does everyone have a guardian angel? And do people with big missions have several guardian angels?

Each of you has a guardian angel in the form of your own Grander Self, just as—for instance—our friend here could be termed the "guardian angel" of his own hand.

However, a big mission is a heavy accomplishment, you might say. And so, there may be several incarnate "hands" on a given piece of equipment at any one time to help move it about. When the job is important and must be done precisely, more than one such as I may oversee and come to help.

You are not so much the handmaidens or handymen of God, as you are the *hands* of God, and the tools by which your Grander Selves effect changes.

If a tool kit had nothing but screwdrivers in it, you would be slow in building your houses. We need the hammers, the protractors, the tape measures, and the saws. We need you to be of different caliber and different sizes in your abilities, interests, and intents—for you do not drive nails with a saw, neither do you cut wood with a hammer. Nor would it do any good for you who are strongly motivated to go against your innate nature and try another course entirely. We know what you are best at, and we are constantly honing you, even as you hone yourselves, to be better at what you do.

This is hard to explain, for in your world, tools remain tools. They are not self-creative in the sense that you are. But you are quite literally tools that transform themselves into their own creations. The best example, perhaps, would be a symphony that constantly refines itself in a composer's mind, playing variations of itself—a never-ending symphony that constantly improves itself in beauty, complexity, and sophistication.

From my point of view, this is an common and ordinary process, but a source of fascination nevertheless. A child may not understand why the adult, when pleased, says, "Wow!" Yet if there were any words you overheard in my reality— spoken by my colleagues, my cousins, my other "guardian angel" friends—the word heard more than any other would be "Wow!"

My only sorrow is to come into a room where you yourselves are not blissed out and blown away by the evident beauty that I perceive—by the enthusiasm, the energies, the glory that is each and every one of you.

Could you describe some of the relationships you have with other Grander Selves?

This is hard to explain in your terms, but I'll try.

Basically, you see, I am a gestalt. And very much more than you individuals do, I find myself giving up or giving *away* parts of my being. The more I fling out of myself, away from myself—renounce, in your terms—the more these renounced aspects of myself spring to an independent life.

It's as if you were a starfish and cut yourself apart, and your limbs and pieces of yourself grew to independent status —not as clones of yourself, but as colleagues. To that degree, we Grander Selves are always meeting up with parts that we abandoned long ago and which are now "grown up."

We forcibly cut ourselves apart, even as we put down air-roots into your reality to form new bodies, new incarnations. Seeing one of those roots being pulled up, you might say, "Ah, he or she is dead!" And yet really, the shoot is being moved and transplanted into yet another field, where it may grow afresh, start its own colony, and send down new air-roots of its own.

We are very much like that: independent living colonies who—though this seems odd to your biologists—can switch our species at will without destroying the integrity of the seeds we have already produced. It's as if a flower in your world were to begin its life as an orchid, then present itself as a rose, and finally become a petunia; yet the seeds produced at every stage remained true to whatever the flower was at that time.

We play with our potential, which is limitless—and that is why we find your reality so fascinating. You are our cold-frame, our greenhouse. You are our flasks, in which we find our being and constantly re-seed ourselves.

Could Grander Selves appear to us as wisps of smoke?

They could appear as giant purple carrots if they so desired. If you saw a talking wisp of smoke, however, you may be less inclined to rush to the psychiatrist!

It depends on how you perceive—or *conc*eive, rather—of non-physical reality. If you have heard of a pillar of smoke by day, or a pillar of fire by night, then that is how you might perceive us with your own senses.

Your preconceptions determine what you perceive in a very direct manner. Thus, to a degree, you perceive any new sort of energy according to your own pre-expectations of it will feel like. Those of you who are content with the energies you know think, "An energy new to me is probably no energy at all"—and those of you who block energies do so for that same reason.

But if you continue to use a new energy, you will find that your preconceptions can alter. You can play with your own preconceptions, using the new energies as a constant. Or, using your preconceptions as constants, you can play with the new energies.

How do you visualize or perceive us?

I will tell you yet another secret about how we discarnates operate. For me, channeling such as you have seen today is very much like being incarnate again. In a sense, it is like putting a paper bag over my head and groping into your human consciousness.

And so, I close our friend's eyes to look through my own. I take the bag off, you might say, and perceive you—even as the sun might perceive the dew in the morning. You are all condensations of the larger field of life-giving "moisture," but from my point of view, I see each of you twinkling with your own reflections.

All of you are separate drops, then—or crystals, or diamonds—each reflecting the light of a different sun, which is your own Grander Self. In that sense, you are your own chandeliers. Each of you catches your Self's clear light, turning it into a myriad of colors, a peacock's tail of blues and oranges and reds and yellows—and other colors that have no names, for your eyes do not have the ability to perceive your own inner radiance.

You are constantly changing, even as the dewdrops change; even as the diamond reflects different aspects of light and of itself, both. This is one reason why on an innate, instinctual level you prize your diamonds so highly. They're fairly common, you know, yet you prize them above all others. Why? Because they constantly change as you look at them. You see diamonds not only as a girl's best friend but as, in a sense, your mineral brothers and sisters.

What is a typical day in the life of a spirit?

There are several answers to that question, just as there are several to what *you* do all day.

When you say "spirit," I infer "one who is between lives," but you are talking about a plural Entity, such as myself . . .What does your stomach do? Your stomach has certain peak hours of activity; and at other times, it goes into quiescence. I perceive "times"—in my terms—when certain of my components or incarnations are active, and times when they are not. Yet in their terms, they are active the *whole* time, just as your stomach is always there, secreting juices and doing its thing quite well, even when you are not aware of it.

To a degree, I am a narrowing or selection of the input available to all my incarnations. It is as if I were working in an audio lab with hundreds of tapes and records to choose from, synthesizing symphonies that you would have great difficulty conceptualizing. I play tapes I've heard before, relive imaginatively—in great emotional and intellectual detail—lives that, in your terms, are fixed in my "past." I whistle possible variations on tunes—in your terms, future existences which I may or may not choose to enter.

As a tree buds and roots, so I expand into various incarnations. I am a tree with the option of growing new roots and branches: My roots go to your past and present, my branches into your future. There are horizontal branches—watershoots— that go sideways into probabilities. I, as a tree, have the option of where I wish to send these extremities: Deciding and doing is what I do all "day."

Time to me is not as it is to you. You consider day and night as approximately 12 hours apiece. To me, a day is as long or short as I need it to be. A thousand years is like a brushstroke of color; yet one day may be the whole rest of the canvas.

I play with, examine, and draw meaning from that which would have no meaning for you. As a musicologist counts the notes in Beethoven and arrives at a hypothesis, so do I "count" such things in your lives as disappointments, headaches and heartaches, aspirations. These form patterns for my—and your —further development. It is not a one-way street, by any means.

When one of your component personalities experiences pain or injury, how does that affect you?

Poolside analogy: You are sitting there, sipping champagne, and you scratch your finger. Your finger feels pain. Does that make you miserable? No, because you perceive the pain in context. You can feel discomfort and not be unhappy. You can feel anxiety and not be depressed.

Do Oversouls deliberately extend personalities to experience poverty and starvation? If so, do efforts to help these people in some way thwart their Grander Selves' intended purpose?

Yes to the first question, no to the second.

As other sources have stated, experiencing negative conditions is not an unmixed curse. Quite often, the individual who undergoes poverty or lack of nourishment is impelled to overcome those conditions in his or her personal future, or in adjacent lives. The love of sharp contrasts demonstrated by your healthy adults should bear out the principle that the experience of extremes is not a human eccentricity, but a drive intrinsic to the Grander Self of which you, as an individual, are a part.

The trick is to meet lack and adversity and fight them—not only on your own behalf, but for others' sake as well. That is, simply amassing a fortune so that you may never again face want is quite praiseworthy, but not the final step. The "next" step— for final steps are as rare in life as they are on the ballet stage —is to provide for others, to "share the wealth" or, more precisely, the means of acquiring that abundance. You need not give away your apples if you distribute their seeds, need not share your catch if you lend your fishing rod.

Can you possibly violate others by wishing to help them? No, *if you do not insist on their accepting your "help" and your help only.* A soul choosing to experience poverty or starvation may be motivated, in part, by the desire to stimulate others' generosity, to open the hearts of others who see life as merely a bed of roses or bowl of cherries. Therefore, by helping those to whom your innate charity directs you, you can play into their hands, as it were, and help fulfill one of the subtler purposes for which they were born in rags and barrenness. As long as your "help" seeks to fulfill, and not distort, the paths those souls have chosen, you will each profit handsomely from the exchange—and not only in material terms.

We Grander Selves take good care of our personalities. Those who are afflicted with disease, accidents, disasters are taken care of. We give you the opportunity for further existences—not because you "have not gotten it right" or have lousy karma. Coming into physical reality, you have taken on a disguise. And you have done so well at your secret-agent assignment that we send you off into yet another mess! We have faith in you. We know that once you get the scary bits out of the way, you may discover that you are in a comedy-adventure, rather than a suspense thriller where the downside is grim indeed. Yes, incarnation is a game, but if it did not seem serious, it would be no game at all. It must be as frivolous as checkers and as maddening as finding yourself beaten at chess, or there would be no point to it. What you enjoy, we enjoy; what you do not enjoy, we learn from.

It is a question of scale and ability. Much of that which you pass by as beneath notice, we find positively enthralling, even as a young child toddles past a Rembrandt that his or her parents stop to admire in awe. Now you see why the parents keep sending the child into the room with the painting, for eventually, child and painting will make a connection.

Why do you Entities keep on reincarnating in physical reality if there are no karmic debts to force you to do so?

Let us try a new analogy: the library.

When you were young, it was tedious for you to learn the alphabet. But once you learned to read, one book led to another. You could "incarnate" your imagination, you might say, in Shakespeare or Jacqueline Susann or whatever book you chose.

Some of you would rather incarnate your imaginations in a non-literary reality—*Dallas*, or *One Life to Live*.

One life gives you the curiosity and the ability to gain nourishment from yet another existence. If you have never read a play, you're going to have problems reading Shakespeare. But with a drama or two under your belt, not necessarily very good ones, then you can ask, "What is *Macbeth* all about?"

Similarly, some of you will say to yourselves—or *have said* to yourselves, or *are saying* to yourselves—"Let's find what the Elizabethan era is all about," or, "I have read that ancient Rome was kind of a gas; let's see!" Out of that curiosity, that intrigue, is born a new life—quite literally, because as soon as you express the desire to know, part of your Grander Self branches out to explore that new area which you *think of* as closed to your knowledge.

One book, one play, may influence you to look into another work by the same writer. Or you may say, "I've read enough of this author—no more of him!" A kind of selection process happens, not only in supermarkets, but in your adjacent lives.

You are fooling yourself if you think that any paths are not enlightened at the end. Enlightenment, progress, and evolution are virtually inescapable. Rationally, that you know if you go to the gym and do so many lifts, your muscles will get a workout and your strength will increase. You *know* that—and yet, over the short term, while you are doing the individual presses, it seems that your muscles are tiring and that you are getting weaker! Lo, you are able to press 100 pounds the first, second, and third times. But on the fourth time, where has your strength gone?

Again, you see, it comes down to a question of scale. Your scientists are delighted to see the sort of patterns that seem to govern atoms come to play again at the macroscopic level of your galaxies. Yet few of your metaphysicians have taken that analogy and seen that what occurs on a small level *morally* is also reflected in the larger, overreaching dimensions of your grander evolution.

It depends which part of the mosaic you choose to look at. When you step back, the pattern emerges. The pattern is delightful, but you cannot create it all at once. You create a masterpiece stroke by stroke—chip by chip, if a mosaic; if a lifetime, day by day and love by love. That analogy will serve you very well indeed.

Do we keep on reincarnating again and again until our souls become perfect?

No! You keep seeding yourself in wider, more advantageous spots. In your terms, you keep transplanting yourself until you find a place where you—*as an individual*, in life or out of it—can begin to expand and grow and form your own "tree."

I will tell you about one of the mistakes I made. My curiosity about the human experience was very deep, and I thought I could not get the whole picture merely by incarnating in the 20th century, in 18th-century Japan, and again in 13th-century Florence. So, about the time of your 15th century, I put all my "fingers" into one bundle and incarnated as three generations of a tribe in Ecuador.

Not every Entity takes on such an assignment, for they find it boring—as if you lived in only one room of a vast mansion, visited an exotic South Seas island and spent all your time in the hotel. Yet you have novelists, painters, sculptors who shut themselves in their studios for days at a time and are blissfully happy. So it was with me, in that circumscribed time and location.

But I learned the hard way not to put all my incarnations in one time-and-space frame. Oh, I understood perfectly what it was like to be that tribe! I experienced life as male and female, old and young, simultaneously. I was able to create vastly fruitful and insightful relationships among my various selves, orchestrating grief against compassion, love against doubt. I was literally the playwright, the play, and the actors. But it was distracting, like listening to a stereo tape where there is only slight divergence between tracks. I could not make a single melody of what I was feeling—whereas it is far easier to harmonize a life of mine in 18th-century Japan with another in 13th-century France.

It sounds like a paradox, yet when two things are too similar, one to the other, it is hard to distinguish them and harder still to make sense of them. My selves crowded one another and could not grow fully. The prohibition against incest, which is endemic through all your cultures, arises from that same perception.

After three generations, I realized that these individual "actors," who had served my purposes so well, deserved to take their own parts—so I struck the set, you might say. And members of that tribe went their individual ways, putting their intents in other times and places—Greece, Rome, Paris, Indochina, and places whose names you know not. Some of them are fairly well advanced at this point and, between lives, are forming Grander Selves all their own.

Even as you are instructed to thin seedlings after you plant them, so I have now learned to be more versatile. Whether you are an individual or a configuration of consciousness, such as I am aspiring to be, you need to keep open the windows of possibility, lest you cloister yourself too narrowly and lose perspective.

(Gesturing:) Why does a banyan tree put down one air-root here and another here, even while it is putting a branch out here? For balance, of course! In your tropics, where the banyan grows, there are monsoons, typhoons, and hurricanes. The banyan has learned, very cleverly, to brace itself against the wind and, by increasing itself, thus escape damage.

We do not grow out of fear; neither do you. We grow to seek opportunity—and so do you. You do not keep going around on the Wheel of Life simply to polish the facets of your character, but because it is enjoyable to do so; and from each part of the circumference, you have a different view. You do not go around on a Ferris wheel for the greater glory of your immortal soul, but because it gives you new views of the city around you. And that is why you go through life after life—it is a pleasure-trip on the Wheel.

I'd like to clarify your image of the banyan tree. Would the main trunk be the Grander Self and the air-roots be its aspects or incarnations?

You could precise-ify it that way if you choose. The banyan does not consider its trunk better than its air-roots, any more than you consider your torso better than your hand. You do not say, "This finger is rather puny compared to my leg, so if it gets lopped off, forget about it—I still have both legs!" So does a banyan tree consider its air-roots a significant part of its being.

If you try to rank portions of your Grander Self on a hierarchy, you'll be shortchanging the *seemingly* less developed

portions—which include yourself! You will have painted
yourself into a corner and must wait for the paint to dry before
you can progress. Do not make that mistake.

I'd rather say the photosynthesizing elements—leaves and
branches—in the sunlight represent your Higher Self. According
to that metaphor, air-roots that come down to earth represent
the manifestations of the Whole Entity in physical reality.
Just as your physical Earth has hard clay, sunlight, and air,
so there are sharp distinctions in the realities I know. Yet it is
no paradox for me to inhabit them all, any more than it is a
paradox for *your* tree to sink its roots in soil and grow leaves
in the air, both. You accept the one idea and, therefore, may as
well accept the other.

You are all connected to the "trunk"—the God-core, if you
will—but hang from different branches of your Grander Selves,
so that you can experience as much as possible of All That Is.

Will we someday know that all you know?

Let's put it this way: We are all on a nature hike. Although
Oversouls may know the names of the trees and be able to
recognize them, yet you incarnates bring us back the leaves
and let us know what is out there.

All is available to you, although when you are focused here,
you do not forget as much as you do not wholly remember.

How do you know when you no longer have to reincarnate on the physical plane?

Having seen a number of springs, summers, falls, and winters pass you by, you reach a point where you no longer *need*
to go out and see the blazing fall foliage or the drifts of new-
fallen snow nestling in the roads. You need not walk out to see
young spring flowers spreading their petals in the April air.
You need not enjoy the Pleiades or the meteor showers, nor
the whisper of winds blowing through branches, now filled
with leaves, that were empty only a few months earlier.

You are not required to do this—but of course, you do!
Your enthusiasms, your sense of celebration and renewal,

send you outdoors to re-commune and re-hook-up with that which you have known before and have learned to love.

What I am saying applies not only to your reincarnations —for you will reincarnate when you *want* to, not when you *have* to—but also to your loves in the here-and-now.

Yet there may come a time when you decide that a relationship has ended, when you tire of the same old view, the harsh winters and cold, clammy climate. And so, you move —to a warmer latitude, to more appreciative arms. As far as your friends left behind are concerned, you are no more; you have removed yourself entirely from the wheel of their seasons. But in fact, you have simply decided to take your marbles to a different playing field.

When you decide to cease reincarnating, it is for a similar reason. You wish to grow orchids or bromeliads, and so, can no longer stand a climate that puts icy frosting on the greenhouse and buries your ambitions beneath a layer of ice.

Desire, enthusiasm, and joy keep you coming back into this world. Desire, joy, and enthusiasm for pleasures quite different will lead you out of it. The earthly objects of your love do not grow stale, but they may indeed be *replaced*— traded in for new models.

Epilogue:

Morning of the Millennium

• The so-called New Age • Whales, dolphins, and human evolution • The lesson taught by errant religious leaders • Duties and functions of spirit guides • Drawbacks of the Ouija board • Benefits of channeling and meditation • Achieving global peace and preserving the natural world • Making your personal world safe and secure • Service to others versus service to self • Spontaneity versus patience • Future architecture in response to breakdown of the ozone layer • On practical brotherhood • The coming—and very gentle!—pole shift

Just a few words, introductorily, on the New Age you have heard so much about. I would suggest that the New Age began this morning!

Every moment of your life begins a New Age. You need not wait for some paradise, for some millennium, for some Messiah —or some old spook such as myself—to lay his benevolent hand on your shoulder and tell you, "Okay, kids, now is the time!"

Recognize that the sunlight coursing through the window is the light of the New Age—which is now. And if you look both without and within, you will see that New Age all around you.

To those who will live a thousand years from now, this age is "the good old days." Yesterday, today was a future you could not totally conceive of. *All* ages are new. Do not worry about waiting until the going gets good, until conditions are right. If they are not yet right, make them so!

It is quite easy to begin living in the world you most fervently desire, simply by accepting nothing less. As I have mentioned many times, precise-ify your desires! There is no time like the present, for indeed, there is no time at all *except* a present which is eternal and extremely responsive to your individual and group desires.

Are whales and dolphins wielding any influence on human consciousness?

Over the centuries, your race has adopted one species or another as an emblem of some quality it felt it lacked. By basking in the quality perceived in that particular beast, your race sought to restore itself to highest equilibrium.

A perfect example is the unicorn. Medieval symbolism was able to create a mentor-animal for itself without having to pin the significance on the donkey, as it were, and infuse with meaning a real-life species from the animal kingdom.

Your current world identifies more closely with the Cetaceae—whales and dolphins—because these mammals are supremely unequipped for war and, though denizens of the sea, breathe the same air as you. Like you, they often fall victim to human beings. And these beasts are rebels: Formerly land animals, they have returned to the same ocean that *apparently* engendered all life forms on your planet. They enjoy a floating, happy existence in tropical waters—their own private hot tub. They toil not, neither do they spin. They eat fish, and some whales are strict vegetarians, straining their own plankton soup. They are laid back, harmless, playful, and extremely intelligent. Many of you even ascribe to them various mystical powers and telepathic abilities!

But if you view them merely as hippies with fins, you miss the point: that human sensitivity to the welfare of other species has increased drastically. Three decades ago, it was still admirable for a Hemingway or a Nabokov to shotgun African mammals or to chloroform scarce alpine butterflies. Nowadays, you try to *increase* the numbers of wildflowers, saltwater fish, and other so-called "wild" species and do not stalk them as members of some alien tribe.

Your allegories switch with the years, for so do your priorities. If the lion and the eagle were once symbols for you to live up to, no wonder both are endangered species!—for even as an animal becomes a conscious emblem of a desired quality among you, so will it thrive and its numbers increase. Hence, the current overpopulation of cats and dogs in cities, where independence and loyalty are in short supply.

Your race will use whatever handholds it can to help it struggle to its feet. If some handholds be merely symbolic—

well, that is okay, too! Dolphins and whales set you a good example, indicating that you can trust an abundant universe to provide you with all you can eat, and that you need not develop technology to become sophisticated and adept.

The Reverend Moon was jailed for tax evasion. The Bhagwan Rajneesh got deported. JZ "Ramtha" Knight was pilloried on TV. Jim Bakker is doing time. Swaggart was caught with his pants down—figuratively and literally. What lesson, if any, were these "religious leaders" trying to teach?

A very important one! Their apparent failures managed to teach you a lesson few of them could easily have articulated, so bound up were they in the misconception of spiritual hierarchy.

For the past few thousand years, spiritual authority has repeatedly been gathered into the hands of an elite few. Had priests of early Christianity not been jealous and possessive, the doctrine that Jesus had died to save mankind would never have been promulgated with such enthusiasm. No religion I could name has not, at one time or another, sought to rescind its Founder's most basic teaching—that the soul has *within itself* the seeds of its own fulfillment and salvation; and that worship of any exterior guru, saint, savior, or deity only prolongs or postpones the eventual task of hauling oneself up by one's own spiritual bootstraps.

Religious "leaders" cannot escape the basic message of your age: that you are *totally* responsible for your own individual salvations. But, as an ancient sage once pointed out, humans are saved as they are! So what, please, is the point of a paid priesthood?

Well, their obvious function is to serve as a repository of disinterested spiritual knowledge—but now, when the tides of individual channeling and self-knowledge are in glorious flood, these religious leaders—*whose unspoken vow it was to lead their "followers" to higher spiritual ground*—are now faced with a rather painful dilemma. How are they to presume to any sort of spiritual authority, when they know perfectly well, in their heart of hearts, that they have no more authority than their followers; that those who follow are possessed of an illusion no less pernicious than the illusion of he—or she—who leads?

And so, they visibly fumble, hoping that you little nincompoops will get the message and pick up the ball for yourselves, without being bidden to do so.

The tragedy of these fallen leaders is that their "failure" was not of grander proportions! In a sense, they were failures chiefly by their *own* standards: They should have viewed their own human "failings" as a diplomatic way of demonstrating that they and their followers are on a totally equal—and totally *comfortable*—footing. Instead, they chose to abdicate entirely, out of a sense of guilt at not having attained the high, and highly unrealistic, goals that their respective belief systems had been preaching. For seldom has a genuine saint been a docile follower of rules and regulations, an obedient worshipper of the status quo.

Has channeling become popular mainly because our religious institutions are spiritually bankrupt?

In your not-so-good old days, each religion was an express train. You had a few engines named Mohammed or Christ or Buddha who had to haul all those poor benighted followers in their wake. Without a very powerful spiritual leader, the Train of Mankind would not move out of the station.

Nowadays, each of you is self-propelled. As a microwave oven accelerates individual molecules, today's spirituality goes direct to where the vibrations are most useful. To get where you want, you don't need to relocate, chant anything, or believe a particular creed. But you *do* need to know where you want to go! Until you turn within, you will find yourself dissatisfied without.

If I have a spirit guide, what are its duties and functions?

You all have spirit guides—to a degree. For the most part, that guide is to you as I am to Tam: namely, a personification or narrowing-down of your Grander Self.

For obvious reasons, an Oversoul cannot afford to debase itself, or it would be no guide. But on the other hand, it cannot be *too* exalted, or there would be very little communication; it would be impossibly distant from the incarnate it was trying to reach. So your guide always stays a few steps out in front, always tempting you forward, always into good.

You have heard me tell you that evil is inability—which your guides fight with the one possible weapon: *ability*. They do not expect you to perform beyond your abilities, so you are taught in increments. Learn to crawl, and you are tempted by seeing others walk. Learn to walk, and you are tempted to run. Run, and you will be tempted to dance.

There are levels of efficiency and grace in spiritual terms also, and you are tempted in those directions by those you perceive to be "centered" or graceful. If you feel envious, you have missed the point: These individuals are merely showing you what you could be like after a workout in the spiritual gym of life.

What you think of as a guide, then, usually works like an automatic transmission, "powered" by the Oversoul. And you are the wheels, which become more efficient as you grow wiser and more fully in tune with your own destiny and abilities. And so, what you perceive as the guide will improve accordingly. It is a simple matter of letting the answers come to you, for if you allow your guide to tempt you onward to grander and more complex lessons, life itself will give you the answers you wish.

The greater the stakes involved, the less the risks. If you *really* desire something, no doubt you will find your way to the goal. Merely pray, "Give us this day our daily challenges . . . and the wisdom to see our assignment for what it is." The rest comes by itself. The child knows it will grow, but you have forgotten that you will continue to grow *forever*.

Not that I look at you as infants. But you know, children build a body from scratch in nine months; can learn any language on earth—sometimes several simultaneously—in two years; and in 10 years can double or triple their body size . . . which few of you adults can do. So if I *compare* you to children, take it as a compliment!

Why are so many people afraid to use the Ouija board?

Sitting down and waiting for messages to be spelled out can be very time-consuming, very tedious. Many would not care to take down even the most fascinating passage if they had to transcribe it letter by letter. When you are adverse to something, fear does not always enter in. Simple affinity or "taste" may be involved, so it is not seemly to accuse others of cowardice if they do not choose to take your dare. They may not be *afraid* of driving 90 miles per hour, but may prefer to walk and enjoy the roadside wildflowers.

Your society puts a premium on speed and efficiency! No wonder vocal channeling has replaced the Ouija, just as radio was welcomed by those impatient with the telegraph. The next step is instantaneous knowing, in which words and conventional concepts are bypassed altogether. Such has been termed "revelation" in your past, but it will take a bit of neurological tinkering before this becomes as widespread a pastime as channeling. So if you wish for inspiration, do not hold your breath—pun intended!

How can I distinguish between my own thoughts and insights, and those promptings and intuitions that arise from my Grander Self?

You are always tapping your unconscious. But whether the thoughts are coming *from* your subconscious or *through* your subconscious is something you can determine only after a bit of investigation.

As I explained, the subconscious is very similar to the eardrum. Sound usually originates outside the ear—but how *far* outside the ear is the question! If you plug one physical ear, you cannot tell where the sound is coming from. Since you have only one subconscious, you do not get "stereo": Any mental voice you may perceive is strictly monaural, you might say. And so, your psyche must learn by experience to tell the difference between a signal that is very close—part of your own thinking—and one that is very far away, or originating from your Grander Self.

Then can our minds learn to make conscious divisions between channeling and intuitive experience?

Conscious divisions are usually thrown up like a barricade, to separate one thing from another. But there *need* not be a division between the phrases you might be able to receive and a more sub-verbal—or supra-verbal—knowing.

You all have experienced the hunch that needs not be corroborated—when you feel a certain knowing in your bones with such clarity and insistence that you need not ask another, much less yourself, the validity of that which you sense innately to be true.

But the intuitive messages you receive are not necessarily from your Grander Self. Rather, as your psi researchers are discovering, *anything* can be channeled—not only an entity but an event, or a relationship. At least three individuals here have, in a situation of romantic confusion, been able to speak eloquently for the relationship that was at risk—and did so to great effect, because relationships often speak louder than the individuals who form them!

An adept or a sensitive—or a listening individual, as most of you are—can bring through an entity such as myself, or the temporarily personalized energy of a relationship or event. But if you listen to *yourself*, you will automatically bring through whatever you need. When a tornado threatens, you will automatically turn on the radio and get the weather report. If presence is needed at home, you will automatically feel the urge to call and check in.

To sum up, your hunches speak to you as eloquently as I ever could. Listen not merely with your ears, but with your heart—indeed, with the whole radius of your energy body that extends outwards in all directions. Once again, you are essentially a sphere of energy 300 feet across, condensed toward the center, with all of your layers picking up different sensations from "out there."

No large amount of these sensations reach your conscious mind, any more than the digestion of your dinner is consciously an issue with you—unless you have indigestion, of course! You are seldom aware of your toes unless someone has stepped on them; similarly, you are more likely to be aware of something when attention needs to be paid to that area.

To digress just a moment, one of the fruits of meditation is that it teaches you to recognize when your body and larger being are running *right*. If you pay attention only to pains and aches and malfunctions, then your body and unconscious become like children who are constantly nagged and corrected, but never praised. Meditation works because it allows you to approve and appreciate your *being* in its naturally healthy state.

Yes, the more you listen—to me or to your own impulses —the more there is to hear and to discriminate among.

Is channeling good for you physically, aside from the spiritual and intellectual stimulation it provides?

Channeling information from the Oversoul level does have specific advantages. By providing this service, you are in touch with a larger, more fully developed version of yourself.

The resulting "influence" is obvious. You will find yourself maturing without growing older. In fact, certain aspects of your physical appearance may well rejuvenate themselves. You will perform certain tasks faster, more efficiently, and vastly *better* than ever before. You will feel a certain confidence—a knowing and loving conspiracy—in the very air you breathe. You will not feel the presence of God, necessarily, but will sense the innate divinity in all things and think of yourself as a fish in a divine river whose substance permeates your body, and in which you swim as your natural environment.

Many of the same virtues are claimed for meditation—but may I suggest that channeling is a slightly more effective way of attaining the same ends? As with meditation, however, it is necessary for a fairly regular—at least once a week—regimen to be set up, for the spirit can be malnourished even as the body can be, if "fed" too infrequently. All in all, this process should bring the practitioner lavish rewards over the long term, quite aside from the satisfaction of curiosity and the stretching of understanding that the new words and concepts provide.

What do I need to do to enhance my spiritual growth?

I could answer that better in a private session, but will widen my answer for general consumption.

Many of you are discouraged by what you see as plateaus or blank walls in your spiritual life—periods of no apparent growth, even backsliding. But simply to consider an example from nature. Even here [*Hawaii*], in a climate where plants *can* grow riotously and joyously the year around, not all of them choose to do so. You will see trees that seem half dead but which, in fact, are merely resting.

One reason a plant will go dormant is to avoid lush, weak growth that is easily broken later. The banana tree, having fruited, is cut down, but from its base come new shoots—often two or three where before, there stood but one.

So it is with your spirituality: Your growth seldom moves in a straight line, at a steady pace. If important areas of your life —or even worse, some of your grandest goals—seem to have died, recognize that they are, rather, in a rest period where they are forming new growth and solidifying gains already made.

Some experiences need to be quietly, leisurely digested so as to make future moves worthwhile. If you find yourselves between romances, that sentence will be of great interest!

Everything follows its own seasons. Your intent to grow, by itself, will keep your spiritual growth flourishing.

For spiritual development, I use a form of Buddhist meditation. From your broader perspective, do you see me making progress?

Any spiritual discipline is a bit like taking vitamins: It does not mean you should stop exercising and watching your diet. At the human level, only one chief method of spiritual development open to you—it is called "daily existence"! If you choose to optimize your existence by meditation, fine! But meditation is only the lubrication for daily life.

Some say that only action—marches, strikes, civil disobedience—can bring about arms control. Others claim that only prayer, meditation, and introspection will lead to world peace. Which approach do you advise?

For the sake of argument, let us compare war to diseases of the body. Now, to combat a given germ, should one spend time in the laboratory investigating immunology and perfecting vaccines? Or should one travel to where the disease is endemic, inoculating, improving sanitation, and imposing quarantines? Both approaches are necessary—neither are they mutually exclusive.

There is no *one* ideal method for stopping a war, any more than there is only one ideal method of fighting one. Your most war-thirsty individuals do their planning in offices where they do not spill a drop of blood. The actual bloodletting is accomplished by those who do little thinking—for someone who troubles to think things through to their final conclusions will seldom want to risk war, the *Bhagavad-Gita* notwithstanding.

A further analogy may help unlock the mental logjam so many of you have constructed around the concept of war: Simply compare it to gambling, for such it basically is. A general dreams of achieving vast tactical goals with a single throw of the dice. Such dreams will keep him expending bullet after bullet in the hopes that the next one may be *the* one, for in his imagination hangs the portrait of someone who broke the bank at Monte Carlo, albeit with a hand grenade.

After all, there *have* been some spectacular wartime winners, as when the A-bomb fell on Hiroshima and the war ended; when Germany pillaged much of the art treasures of Europe scarcely more than a century after Napoleon had done the same; when the Americans won independence from Britain and the French won independence from themselves. But with any such victory, the unpublicized losses—in terms of suffering, in terms of lost opportunities for growth *on the part of the victor*—are overwhelming.

If you would seek peace, you may of course meditate or march, pray or protest, as your conscience moves you. But I suggest a third and truly revolutionary course of action. Devise a means of accomplishing the same ends which war and violence only *seem* to effect so easily. Only the victorious soldier is truly happy, but a man working at some fulfilling task will be happy most of his day and bring to his task a loyalty and dedication that any military commander would envy. Individuals can always turn aside violence—simply because violence must be a group effort. Armies numbering fewer than six are traditionally looked upon with some derision, but the brilliant innovator requires no quorum to do his thing. The solitary individual who helps others prosper, captures the imagination just as vividly as the soldier who single-handedly "surrounded" a platoon of German soldiers.

The same instinct that drives mobs can inspire them to challenges of a more beneficial nature, where there *need* be no loser in order for there to be victors. And by your own private seeking for solutions, you will use up some of the personal energy and aggression that you might otherwise expend in a preemptive first strike—if only in word or thought—against that idiot who just cut you off on the freeway.

How can we resolve our desire for economic growth and the need to preserve a beautiful, unspoiled, healthy environment?

The easiest way to ensure your environment's preservation is to make its continued protection economically rewarding. Not an easy task, but establishing natural parks and hiking trails, photographers' wildflower preserves, rural summer writers' colonies—any of these would provide an effective start.

Too often, your planners forget that roads and buildings, quite unlike mountains and valleys, do not automatically renew themselves, but must be placed on a "life support system" paid for by surrounding inhabitants. Did you appreciate more fully the thrift and economy of the natural world, your businessmen would seek to harness its methods of productivity; and you would not be in such a rush to "develop" land. Rather, you would strive to assist the land in its *own* development—toward greater fertility, or as the selected habitat for given species. No tract of acreage, however dry and barren, will not respond to human energy in its quest to achieve its own highest potential.

And once you have experienced that response—have come to realize that the land itself is conscious, with a will and life of its own—then you will view your bulldozers and steamrollers in a wholly different light! And given that recognition, a new non-exploitative partnership with the land will follow automatically.

Should we make efforts to imagine a better society, or is that the same as just wishful thinking?

Wishful thinking is not *inherently* different from pure, free acts of creative imagination. Yet the two are qualitatively different, of course, for you may rehearse in imagination acts

and events that you would not care to have occur in real life—
and that form of thinking could hardly be called wishful.

As I said earlier, even the most vivid dress rehearsal does
not guarantee that the play you envision will ever see opening
night, much less succeed with its intended audience. To
return to the wording of your question, it is hard to imagine
a better society *in its entirety*. It is far easier to imagine a better
neighborhood—a more loving and fulfilled family; a more
peaceable, creative, supportive street—than to conjure up
vague ideas of peace and prosperity for your planet as a whole.
How does one precise-ify the image of a world at peace,
except symbolically? The image of a world at war is far more
vivid and easy to hold in your imagination.

Your best bet is to imagine how your daily round may best
be integrated with the better society you hope for. If you view
your personal accomplishments as indispensable ingredients in
a better world—*imagining as precisely as you can how you can
thus contribute, and exactly how your efforts hook up with
society at large*—you will be well on your road to a better
world.

A serious misconception keeps you from achieving everything you can: You fear that any potential Utopia is an all-or-
nothing proposition; that as long as one individual suffers
poverty, ill health, or injustice, then the whole society must
suffer. On one level, that is certainly true. Yet just as a healthy
society may harbor pockets of backwardness and ignorance,
so may superiority of whatever stripe break out spontaneously
in the midst of prevailing mediocrity—and grow simply by
inspiration and example!

Such a "blemish of excellence" was ancient Athens, was
Renaissance Florence, was colonial Philadelphia, and are your
various artists' colonies today. A few miles in either direction, individuals look on the arts with scorn. Yet they in no way
prevent the existence—or persuasiveness—of excellence, any
more than the heat of your oven prohibits ice cubes in your
freezer, only a few feet away.

Of course your universe is interconnected, so that developments in one part directly affect every other. But as in biology,
you have semi-permeable membranes. As in electronics, you
have different forms of insulation that allow individuals—and

individual *abilities*—to develop in a relative isolation that contributes to their growth. Geologic crystals, to further that example, could not assume their distinctive perfection except in a relatively pure solution of their component mineral. Just so, artists and writers need to isolate themselves, often with the telephone unplugged, for their brain children to come to full term.

In many ways, products and insights engendered during your retreats rejuvenate and refresh the everyday life from which you were taking a vacation. Suppose you were a red blood corpuscle, coursing through overtired muscle tissue. You would be eager to reach the lungs and exchange those carbon dioxide molecules for the life-giving oxygen that you yourself need to survive. But on your return, your own renewed presence would assist measurably in that overworked muscle's recuperation.

So by withdrawing temporarily from the shortcomings of your fellow beings, you can benefit them more directly and *practically* than if you kept vigil over their sufferings. Such "retreats" are in no way cowardly. And if you infuse your daily experience with your own unique personality, *and then imagine that experience being plugged into your larger society in ways with which you are already familiar,* your nourishment of the larger world will automatically take care of itself.

Not that you should hesitate to act when you feel the need, but never hesitate to daydream on the most intimate and immediate level. The fulcrum by which the Earth may be shifted lies ever at your feet or, at the furthest, at your doorstep. And if you think of the multitude of *individuals* whose dreams have altered your world for the better, you can more easily envision how the local excellence that you create can spread far beyond the circumference of your conscious control.

What is the most constructive way of protecting one's home from disaster?

Calamities that affect houses are quite often the result of conflicted or blocked desires that might otherwise afflict the body. What happens to your home need *not* happen to you, and vice versa—though neither should become the whipping

boy for the other. But if you see your body as evil or disobed-
ient, you may seek to "punish" your home instead. And if
your home is a place of discord and argument, of fear and
resentments, you will inevitably attract forces to discharge the
negative energies that have seeped into the walls.

If you feel the place has been psychically "contaminated"
by a previous tenant, there is no need to move out. Even as
linen smells fresh after a few hours of blowing in a sunny wind,
so can any dwelling be purged and mentally fumigated by
conscious applications of love and appreciation for all connected with it—from the builder on up; for it is hardly right to thank
All That Is for your daily bread and then neglect to thank
the farmer who was instrumental in getting those loaves to you
in the first place.

You have an old saying that there is safety in numbers.
Simply speaking, objects in physical reality enjoy greater duration if their continued existence benefits a great many *diverse*
people. The destruction of monuments beloved of one sect or
nationality is often the physical outbreak of confused tensions
and repressed doubts about the group identity. But a given "object" beloved of all ages, races, and classes will tend to stay in
good shape.

While it would not improve the safety of your home to
invite an entire throng to dwell within its walls, it is effective to
make your home's undamaged existence of benefit to as many
others as possible. Even if you are a stickler for privacy, make
at least one room of the house—or even better, one spot in
each room—a place where intangible entities of good will can
visit to refresh themselves. Such a "place" can be as modest as
a vase of flowers or as sophisticated as an array of Renaissance bronzes. Invite whichever benevolent discarnates you
hold in greatest esteem to come and partake of the beauty
you have assembled, and you will have less to worry about in
terms of lightning, earthquake, and the like.

The idea is to see "your" house not as yours exclusively,
but as a temporary dwelling that, in some distant year, you intend to bequeath to others who will follow you upon Earth—
together with the furnishings and "good will" you have built
up within it. It helps, too, to think of human visitors to your
home as ones who need a spiritual pit stop, to be refueled and

refreshed by whatever "good vibes" are intangibly but unmistakably in the air. And so, by using your shelter as a tool to a higher purpose, you in effect bribe the universe to keep it in good shape for you *and for all others* who partake of what it has to offer.

Those who live in places where tornadoes and tidal waves wreak their toll, do so for their own personal reasons. You will notice that great learning and culture seldom arise in areas threatened by natural cataclysm. Communities stricken by flood, tempest, and fire are too often stagnant: Mental and physical underbrush needs be cleared away so that future entities dwelling in that place can have elbow room and breathe freely.

To a degree, your San Francisco has avoided even stronger earthquakes by dedicating itself so strongly to the future. Rather than hoard up treasures and accomplishments of the past, that city's inhabitants pride themselves on being forerunners and pioneers in life-style, consciousness, and discovery. No need for an earthquake to "shake them up a bit," if they are already expending energy that the Earth might otherwise need to release for them.

And so, if you would have a secure home, then love the future well enough not to fear it. That way, your home can slide forward into an era on which you have envisioned the outlines of a new Golden Age in which any being would feel privileged to live.

Know, too, that visitors who come to see you are visiting a special place. It is your loving duty to *keep* it special, in quiet and subtle ways that their spirits—primarily—can appreciate. And so, these visitors, visible and otherwise, will share your best wishes for the continued security of your floor, walls, and roof.

If all souls are sparks of God, and all beings ultimately one, then is service to others any different from service to self?

Each pole of service—to others or to self—represents an extreme of what you think of as cooperation, which is the natural state of all existence.

You have a familiar saying that one hand washes the other. A single hand would find it difficult to perform service-to-self, nor can a hand wash its brother or sister hand without coming clean in the process. However, you may not perceive the direct benefits to self inherent in serving others, nor see clearly how *you* benefit others by keeping yourself healthy and well-supplied.

On a perfectly straight road, you would be able to drive directly toward your destination with nary a swerve. But because physical reality is a winding road—picturesque, if you choose to look on the bright side—you need to make any numbers of turns, switchbacks, and other corrections along the way. *Pure* service to others and *pure* selfishness, so-called, might best be thought of as hard left-hand and hard right-hand turns. Only if you continue making them do you wind up going in circles. And only if you forget your further goals do you continue making them in the first place.

Why is patience a virtue? Aren't spontaneous impulses the signals for actions best suited to us?

"Virtue" implies a form of moral superiority. Why not re-define it as *opportunity*?

Let's say you are presented with a painting you have never seen before. You consider that it is not to your liking, and turn your gaze to another canvas. But if you are an art dealer, your eye will linger longer, sizing up the work's condition and whether it would be worth acquiring for re-sale. If you are an artist, you may take ten minutes to mentally re-paint the picture in your imagination, combing through it for techniques and effects you can appropriate for your own work.

Now, which of these three examples has been most patient? All have been *equally* so, for each individual has turned away from the painting as soon as his curiosity was finally satisfied. "Patience" is involved only when the universe insists that there is more to meet your eye than you have assumed; and so a given set of circumstances remains on the "screen" of your slide lecture longer than you might like—but only so that you have a better chance to grasp the lesson it offers.

Of course, change is not *always* beneficial. Sometimes the bell rings and brings the class to an end before the students have grasped all that they came there to know. Sometimes, a given picture puzzle or test question is withdrawn because the student cannot "get" it, and can spend the remaining time more profitably on other material.

In short, when time seems too long, take a second look —or a third. If you have indeed gotten from these enduring circumstances everything you can, then why are they still enduring?

Your own impatient curiosity is a most powerful force for change and is impeded only when, on a deeper level, you feel you must take a closer, more leisurely look.

When psychologist Helen Wambach progressed hypnotized subjects forward in time, many described Earth's inhabitants in 2100 A.D. living underground or housed in above-ground domes that—it was implied—shielded them from high levels of radioactivity prevailing outside. If this preview of the future is valid, how might we build such domes?

The technology currently used to erect geodesic domes would be all you need to build such structures. But the corroborative nature of these hypnotized subjects' accounts raises a deeper question that I should address, lest you gather up potentially false information about your so-called future. Much of your extrasensory researches into the past and present are contaminated by this Piggy-Back Syndrome.

If misinformation creeps into your credit file or medical records, that erroneous data will be "perceived" by anyone who looks into the file. Sometimes, as you know, it takes years to correct such errors which, in the meantime, are accepted as valid simply because they appear in the file.

Now, thoughts are indeed things, and *any* perception made in trance takes on a life of its own—if only because it is held in the memory bank of the individual doing the hypnotizing or the research. When asked to obtain telepathic information to which it does not normally have access, the unconscious mind that is not trained in these skills readily reaches for whatever thought is near to hand—*as long as it is identified as being "other" and not a product or projection of its own.* Therefore, it is all too easy to seize on a thought held by the hypnotist and perceive it—simply because it is external to the self—as "fact."

This whole process is actually a kind of proof of the existence of telepathy, then, and in no way counts as a refutation. Not that the hypnotist is controlling the shots. Rather, amateur psychics tend to grope for answers that have *already* been judged acceptable. They seize on the tried and true, you might say—and obviously, the answers nearest to hand are ones provided by *previous* psychics. And retracing an existing error only deepens and enlarges it.

In the incident you speak of, the subjects were picking up—and reinforcing one another's impressions of—a probable future in which inhabitants chose to avoid the unshielded rays of the sun. Their domes were intended to filter out some of the less beneficial spectra of *solar* radiation, which some of the hypnotized interpreted as "radiation," period.

Your scientists have already discovered that plants grow better when "deprived" of some of sunlight's more destructive rays, which optical fibers can filter out. Your future-glimpsers, then, were seeing a dome that acted as does a cloudy overcast, softening and filtering the sunlight. At the time of Wambach's experiments, there was already worry that your ozone layer might decay, letting through destructive components of sunlight. This fear helped form—or rather, *select*—the probable future upon which the subjects tended to seize.

How can you explore your reality without becoming entangled in the bleedthroughs of others' concepts, fears, and personal interpretations? Simply desire that thought-forms left by any other sentient being shall not "register" upon your inner senses, and ask that you will perceive only that which is strictly accurate. Such an approach may still give you pieces of conflicting testimony, for your society places great store on uniformity, corroboration, and "supporting testimony"—which of course explains why the unconscious so gratefully accepts ideas that have been previously endorsed in some way. Thus, to accurately perceive your *own* future, your *own* impressions, may take a little doing.

True clairvoyance depends on being able to see *through*, see *past* whatever perceptual grids your fellow men have scribbled on the windows through which they view external reality. Too often, you take pictures with your own camera, so to speak, but use society's tripod, which is already aimed at a predetermined sight. Often—to follow the analogy—you adopt the same *f/*stop and shutter speed as your neighbors who took the same shots. Just as parallax is necessary to determine the true dimensions of distant objects, so are differing interpretations vital if your society is to appreciate the full richness and multiplicity of the realities—and by extension, options—available to you.

How can we best achieve the universal brotherhood that so many teachers and visionaries have foreseen?

In your lexicon, the term *brotherhood* has taken on a certain tarnish, largely because it has been overextended—and, on the other hand, not extended far enough.

Too often, the concept of brotherhood has required that one simply close one's eyes to differences and idiosyncrasies in other men and women or, worse, invite indiscriminately into one's heart every single member of the human species. And so, brotherhood has come to seem a hopelessly lofty and rarefied goal for which one should strive, but need not really attain.

I would like to change all that by pointing out that brotherhood is a concept you can use for immediate, personal, and highly *practical* results. I will further shake up your sensibilities by suggesting that your concept of brotherhood should extend far beyond your own species. Even the sidewalk that supports you and the gravity that keeps the air dense enough to breathe are your "brothers"—in the sense Saint Francis gave the term—teaming up with you to create the universe you know.

Just as a child needs to rebel in order to achieve independence, so you for many centuries warred among yourselves—so that human consciousness could expand more fully than in a "warm and happy family" and literally colonize as many differing points of view as possible. Similarly, in your so-called corporate jungles, it may well appear that the most aggressive individual gets the best job, the most perks. And yet, to make my point crystal clear, suddenly subtract all the other workers in the company! In total isolation, even the most self-promoting individual could do very little to fulfill his ambitions.

I am not asking you to ignore the faults you believe you perceive in others, nor am I authorizing snobbery or clannishness of any stripe. I *am* suggesting that you broadcast a general feeling of trust—an assumption that every object and individual, animate and inanimate, in your world is directly striving for a better, more fulfilling existence *for all concerned.* If you like, think of the poor as gallantly enduring poverty to help stretch the consciences of those more fortunate. Think of microbes and vermin as providing goads toward medical research and improved sanitation. See the rot that crumbles a fine building as opening the way for the construction of one even more lovely. And trust that Nature, in her infinite variety, will swiftly grow to heal whatever scars Man has inflicted on her.

The attitude I am recommending is actually quite widespread in the animal and plant kingdoms, and accounts for what some of your scientists have identified as sociobiology—as the sacrifice of one individual for the sake of its species. In reality, Nature knows no such thing as sacrifice. One individual—one species, even—may step aside and lend the stage to another, but with the tacit understanding that it may have the floor back at some later time, in some later incarnation. Your naturalists will continue to be puzzled by the persistent, often stubborn reappearance of solitary representatives of species hitherto believed extinct. These are simply harbingers of their species, waiting somewhat impatiently in the wings for their cue to come flooding back *en masse* into the spotlight. Therefore, I am simply advocating that you adopt a general assumption or root belief that your planet's life forms have long used— and to excellent advantage.

Once you identify every facet of your world as a co-worker toward an existence more various and fulfilling than you can imagine, your own role will automatically adjust itself. You will see *yourself* as a worker—a part-timer, to be sure—in the shaping of other people's lives. And you will want to seize each precious chance to invest the vacant moments of the day with extra love, cheer, humor, and help.

In helping others, you will not exhaust your own resources, nor promulgate others' interests at the expense of your own. Rather, as if by magic, you will find yourself and the universe pulling in the same direction in any number of endeavors—because the more you sense yourself a contributing part of the world, the more *your* world will tame itself to your specifications and literally bud with fruit and flowers to your personal taste. Others will discard, for free, that which you most desire. Again and again, you will find yourself "getting a break" where none could have been anticipated. And you will find painless—indeed, quite enjoyable—opportunities to help others in their private spheres of influence.

In implementing this exercise, it may help to use a form of animism. Imagine the shoes on your feet, the winds that sweep across the other side of the globe, the stars several billion light years out, and the dead leaves scampering across the lawn as all having their own specific purpose. You need not stop to define that purpose. Merely trust that there *is* one and that it acts in your highest interest. That trust is the basis of true brotherhood, for how can you accept another object or species, let alone another human being, if you harbor fear that it or it, he or she secretly wishes to flourish at your expense? And if you think that *you* must grow at anyone else's expense, what a sad task it is to sort those whom you must injure and ignore from those whom you perceive as "our kind"!

Those of a cynical and pragmatic nature can simply place the universe on the honor system—and will be quite astounded at the rapidity and thoroughness with which the universe moves to fulfill the trust they had hesitated to extend, the hopes they had long buried as being too impractical.

Many psychics are predicting that the Earth's poles will shift around the turn of the century. If so, how can we increase our chances of survival?

Just as you have myths that you project into the past, so are certain myths projected forward into your future—across the mists of time, where they may be seen as comfortably divorced from present-tense reality. The axis-shift "prophecies" are simply that: myths which, like pearls, have built up rather splendid and shimmering layers over a core grain of truth.

Then do you predict that the pole shift will not occur?

True, the Earth has changed its axis of rotation many times during the course of its revolutions through space, and will again—largely because of the unequal weight caused by mountain-building. Note that most of your mountain chains are balanced on either side of the equator, not toward the high poles. But the prediction of a *sudden* shift, of devastating tidal waves and other catastrophic phenomena, is largely a product of Man's imagination.

Have you ever observed a spinning top as it begins to slow down? You will notice that it loses its uprightness gradually. It takes a great many revolutions for the toppling top's previous axis—which was pointing upright at the moment of initial spin—to become its "equator." So it will be when the Earth next changes its axis, though of course the Earth will not slow its spin, as the top does.

The beginning of the change will be hardly perceptible. As the wobble slowly increases—becoming noticeable only after a couple of years—the transition will still be gradual. The disruption of normal ocean and atmospheric convections will cause storms, but nothing wildly out of the ordinary. The main "disaster" will be in the distortion of previously valid methods of navigation, and in the disruption of biological timetables in the natural world. Indeed, one of the "purposes" of this shift is to reclaim for a future world land that, because of present climate patterns, is now desert or semi-arid. Another purpose is to render technology just inaccurate and unreliable enough that Man is forced to fall back on the instinctual abilities that are his birthright and not the patented prerogatives of any particular culture.

Now, why has the axis shift gained such a prodigious hold on your collective imaginations? Simply because it is symbolic of a greater, deeply felt truth: The world of the future will "revolve" on a different basis than the one you know today.

A society, the lifespans of whose individuals are finite, always sees transformation as spelling the death of the present generation, the end of an era—and, therefore, as catastrophe. Now, there is a growing dissatisfaction with the world you have built and the rules you abided by during its building. And because

Man often tears down completely, to build upon a fresh foundation scoured out of the depth of the earth, you naturally assume that the universe is similarly inclined to "clear the decks" and start with a clean slate. Yet anyone who has watched the sneaky arrival of spring will know how the universe goes about its transformations and renewals—subtly, irresistibly, and with a fragrant charm that not even the most conservative can begrudge.

So yes, in your *very* far distant future, look for the stars above your heads to swim on different arcs. Look for your not-so-distant future world to revolve on a different axis—of beliefs and intent, of priorities and equalities. And please understand that if the enormous weight of the ice caps during your last ice age did not cause a realignment of the poles, your present rather puny South Polar accumulation will not do the trick. Your Earth bulges along its equator like a well-fed burgher, and the angular momentum built up over centuries would take at least a decade to realign.

To survive any axis shift, you need only "survive" each day to the best of your ability. A day spent in deepest health and joy tends to beget other such days. The best preparation for a dry, lean season is moderate consumption and temperate, confident living—not gorging, running to hide in a cave, or in otherwise distorting your behavior in anticipation that hard times ahead will "correct" your present imbalances for you.

Nature always allows for a certain leeway in your fortunes, and a simple orientation toward health and general fulfillment will automatically protect you in your comings and goings upon *this* Earth—or any future one.

About the Editor

Tam Mossman graduated from Yale University in 1967. As a Senior Editor at Prentice-Hall, he contracted and edited such best sellers as *W.C. Fields by Himself* and *The Amityville Horror*, as well as the work of Jane Roberts—from *The Seth Material* through her posthumously published *Dreams, "Evolution," and Value Fulfillment*.

In 1975, he first made contact with his own Grander Self, James, who has been quoted in Jon Klimo's *Channeling* and Michael Talbot's *Your Past Lives*. In 1985, he founded *Metapsychology*, a 96-page quarterly evoted to exploring the operation of consciousness outside the physical body.

(Back issues are still available. For a sample copy and detailed list of contents, send $4.95 to Tiger/Maple Press, Box 36, Cave Creek, AZ 85331.)

Self-employed as a securities analyst, he recently finished a two-act stage adaptation of John Milton's *Paradise Lost*, and is compiling a new book of James's explanations and exercises.

If you've enjoyed this book . . .

you can order extra copies for yourself or a friend—and take a ten percent discount!

Mail to: **Tiger/Maple Press**
P. O. Box 36
Cave Creek, AZ 85331

Please send me ___ copy(ies) of *Answers from a Grander Self* at $11.65 each, postpaid. ($13.90 each if sent to an address in Canada. Arizona residents please add 5.5% sales tax.) I enclose a check or money order for _____, payable in U.S. funds.

Name: _____

Address: _____

City: _____ State: _____ Zip: _____

Mail to: **Tiger/Maple Press**
P. O. Box 36
Cave Creek, AZ 85331

Please send me ___ copy(ies) of *Answers from a Grander Self* at $11.65 each, postpaid. ($13.90 each if sent to an address in Canada. Arizona residents please add 5.5% sales tax.) I enclose a check or money order for _____, payable in U.S. funds.

Name: _____

Address: _____

City: _____ State: _____ Zip: _____